Tales from the Seattle Mariners

KIRBY ARNOLD

SportsPublishingLLC.com

ISBN-10: 1-58261-831-3
ISBN-13: 978-1-58261-831-9

Publishers: Peter L. Bannon and Joseph J. Bannon Sr.
Senior managing editor: Susan M. Moyer
Acquisitions editor: John Humenik
Editor: Doug Hoepker
Art director: K. Jeffrey Higgerson
Cover design: Joseph Brumleve
Project manager: Kathryn R. Holleman
Photo editor: Erin Linden-Levy

Sports Publishing L.L.C.
804 North Neil Street
Champaign, IL 61820
Phone: 1-877-424-2665
Fax: 217-363-2073
www.SportsPublishingLLC.com

Printed in the United States of America

Library of Congress Cataloging-in-Publication Data

Arnold, Kirby, 1954-
    Tales from the mariners dugout / Kirby Arnold.
    p. cm.
Includes index.
    ISBN-13: 978-1-58261-831-9 (hard cover : alk. paper)
    ISBN-10: 1-58261-831-3 (hard cover : alk. paper)
    1. Seattle Mariners (Baseball team)--Anecdotes. I. Title.
GV875.S42A76 2007
796.357'6409797772--dc22
                                   2007007538

This book is dedicated to my family, which has encouraged and supported me from the day I wrote my first word as a sportswriter.

To my father, whose love of baseball left a permanent imprint on me.

To my mother, who drove me from ballpark to ballpark after I landed my first newspaper job as a 15-year-old without a driver's license.

To my two children, who are the delights of my life.

And most of all, to my wife for her unending love and support of my passion, despite the hours she spent waiting for me in empty high school gyms and the nights at home alone as I worked.

I am truly privileged.

—KA

CONTENTS

CHAPTER ONE

Baseball in Seattle

WILL IT FLY, OR FLY AWAY?

LEE ELIA NEEDED HIS PREGAME CIGARETTE, so he ducked into a hallway outside the Seattle Mariners' clubhouse and lit up.

It was less than an hour before a weeknight game in September, typically an empty-house night in the vast Kingdome. Elia, the Mariners' hitting coach, was puffing away that 1995 evening when he peered through an opening that gave him a good view of the stadium. What he saw stunned him.

"My God," Elia said to himself. "This place is filling up."

He walked back inside the clubhouse and stopped Sam Mejias, the Mariners' first-base coach.

"Hey Sammy, do we have a promotion tonight?" Elia asked.

"I don't think so, Lee," Mejias answered. "Why?"

"Well," Elia said, "that's not our usual 12 or 13 thousand out there. This place is filling up."

It was a trend in the making. By September of 1995, there was no such thing as a typical weeknight in the Kingdome. The Mariners had found some magic on the field, climbing from 13 games out of first place in the American League West Division in mid-August to contention by mid-September, and they'd done it with a series of two-out rallies and comeback victories that created a buzz in Seattle. For the first time ever, baseball became important in September, and big crowds were watching the Mariners in the Kingdome.

"We went back out a little later to take infield practice, and I noticed a little guy out in center field who was holding a sign," Elia said. "It read, 'Refuse to Lose.'"

Those words became the Mariners' battle cry.

"I was telling guys, 'Look at that: Refuse to Lose. You know what? The way we're playing, we might not lose this thing,'" Elia said. "I think that night there must have been 30,000 people at that game, and the energy was terrific. You could feel it in the clubhouse, and it never stopped."

Two weeks later, the Mariners were still refusing to lose and, best of all, their growing fan base was on board for a delirious ride that helped prove Seattle is indeed a baseball town. The city had suffered through the loss of the Seattle Pilots after one season in 1969, then nearly two decades of losing seasons and meaningless Septembers by the Mariners. But suddenly, Seattle found baseball worth celebrating.

The Mariners went on to win the '95 American League West Division championship, beating the California Angels 9-1 in a one-game tiebreaker on October 2. Across the Pacific Northwest, fans reveled over what their team had accomplished. They sported their Mariners hats with pride, and purchased jerseys with the names Griffey, Martinez, Buhner, Johnson, Wilson, Cora, and Piniella on the back. For those final weeks of September, then six playoff games in October, cheering inside the Kingdome had never been louder for baseball, and the enthusiasm throughout the Northwest had never been greater for the Mariners.

Those who had proclaimed for years that Seattle wasn't a baseball town—and there were plenty—couldn't say that anymore. It only took the Mariners 19 years to prove every naysayer wrong. Since 1977, winning a championship seemed like the remotest of possibilities.

The Mariners were known better for goofy promotions like "Funny Nose Glasses Night," which drew a bigger crowd to the Kingdome in 1982 than Gaylord Perry pitching for his 300th career victory did just two nights earlier. Over their first few years, the Mariners offered some memorable moments on the field as well as players who became fan favorites. Their fans cheered good young players such as center fielder Ruppert Jones and second baseman

Julio Cruz; but fans also appreciated a prankster like Bill Caudill, a solid closer who had earned the nicknames "The Inspector" and "Cuffs," because of his penchant for handcuffing unsuspecting victims—including the owner's wife.

Anyone who followed the team in the early years learned not to expect too much, especially late in the season when the games held little meaning. Before 1995, the Mariners were known for small crowds in the Kingdome, where the sound of cheers lingered only because the huge concrete structure allowed plenty of room for echoes to reverberate.

Yet the infant Mariners endured through shaky ownership and fears that they would follow the fate of the Pilots and move to Seattle. Star players like Alvin Davis, Mark Langston, Harold Reynolds, Omar Vizquel, Ken Griffey Jr., Randy Johnson, Jay Buhner, Alex Rodriguez, and Edgar Martinez wouldn't come along to pique anyone's interest until years later. The early Mariners were a tough sell to the fans, and winning over the media wasn't any easier.

The Struggle for Respect

Randy Adamack was 27 when he joined the Mariners midway through their second season, 1978, as public relations director. He spent many of his first days on the job introducing himself to the media, and among his appointments was a meeting with Georg Meyers, the former sports editor of the *Seattle Times*. The two talked for a few minutes, and Adamack remembers feeling good about how Meyers received him. The man was pleasant and cordial, and he seemed willing to give baseball a chance, Adamack thought. Then Meyers bluntly ended the meeting with the absolute truth.

"Randy, you seem like a nice young man, and I wish you a lot of success," Meyers said. "But I have absolutely no interest in baseball. Good luck."

Welcome to Seattle. Have fun trying to make baseball work here. Don't let the football season hit you on the backside.

"There wasn't a lot of inherent media interest in this town," Adamack said.

But did that mean this wasn't a baseball town? As far back as 1903, Seattle was considered an important piece of the newly formed Pacific Coast League, and the city maintained a rich minor-league heritage with the PCL into the 1960s.

"More often I heard, 'Can Seattle be a baseball town?'" Adamack said. "I tried to get myself up to speed on the history of baseball in Seattle. There is a baseball background here, but would that translate to Major League Baseball?"

Nobody would be able to answer that for years.

"We hoped baseball would work and we certainly wanted to give it a chance to do so," Adamack said. "But I don't think it was ever really tested until many years later. Anything above a .500 record became the goal for us. It wasn't like that was the end-all. But you've got to walk before you run, and we hadn't even walked yet."

Only the most positive thinkers back then could have imagined a season like 1995 happening in Seattle. In fact, only the most positive could have imagined baseball lasting that long in the city. The 1969 Seattle Pilots, an expansion team doomed by ownership problems, a small old outdoor ballpark, and little talent on the field, played just one season in Seattle. Sick's Stadium, built for minor-league baseball in 1938 and expanded for the Pilots, was supposed to be a temporary home until construction of a new domed stadium, approved by voters in 1967, was completed in 1972. Despite playing in a ballpark with poor sight lines and plumbing problems, the Pilots actually drew more fans to their home games in 1969 than four other major-league teams. Still, Sick's Stadium was inadequate by major-league standards, and team owners dealt with serious financial problems.

During the off-season before the 1970 opener, attempts to keep the Pilots in the hands of local ownership failed, as did lawsuits to prevent anyone from moving them out of Seattle. Bud Selig bought the team, moved it to Milwaukee, and renamed it the Brewers.

Jack Aker, a pitcher who played less than two months with the Pilots before they traded him to the Yankees, hated seeing that.

"The fans in Seattle were very enthusiastic, win or lose," Aker said. "There was never any booing. They were just happy to have a team. I thought it would work if they would get a new stadium."

The last-place Pilots likely would have faded into obscurity if not for one thing: Pitcher Jim Bouton wrote a book—*Ball Four*—which became a bestseller for its revealing look at the quips, quirks, and escapades of Bouton and his Seattle teammates.

Many prominent Seattle civic leaders were not willing to allow *Ball Four*—or the failure of the Pilots—to become their city's baseball legacy. Local government leaders, many of whom had fought major-league owners to keep the Pilots, began a new battle to reinstate Seattle as a major-league city. A lawsuit challenging baseball's antitrust laws became the impetus for the expansion season of 1977, when Toronto and Seattle were added to the American League.

The Mariners were born.

The notion that Seattle could succeed as a major-league city would take a while.

Would Anybody Support a Losing Team?

Many believed Major League Baseball wouldn't work a second time in Seattle, and in the early years the Mariners didn't do a lot to dispute their argument. They averaged 89 losses their first 18 seasons, lost more than 100 games three times and, just when they seemed to have turned a corner with their first winning record—83-79—in 1991, the Mariners followed it with a 98-loss, last-place season in 1992.

Even those in the Mariners' front office weren't sure if Major League Baseball would work.

"I wondered about it myself all the time," said Lee Pelekoudas, the traveling secretary in 1979.

In a city where football was king and the Seahawks drew capacity crowds to the Kingdome on Sundays, baseball was often filler on the sports calendar. The National Basketball Association Sonics occupied the winter months, and the Mariners drew intrigue, if nothing else, when their season started in April. But when mid-July rolled around and the Mariners found themselves hopelessly out of contention, interest shifted back to football and the Seahawks' training camp.

On September weeknights in the early years, the Mariners were lucky to draw 5,000 to a game.

"I remember a game against Cleveland when somebody hit a foul ball into the stands down the left-field line next to the bullpen," Pelekoudas said. "Nobody went down to get it. Everybody was sitting behind the plate between the dugouts."

Former Mariners shortstop Julio Cruz, who became one of the first fan favorites off the original 1977 team, didn't sense an overwhelming wave of support in the early years.

"On the streets, you never saw anything that advertised the Mariners," he said. "It wasn't like it is now, when you see Mariners jackets and hats and shirts everywhere you go. Now there are posters of the guys on buses."

Play-by-play announcer Dave Niehaus, the voice of the Mariners since the first game in 1977, suffered through more losses than anyone with the ballclub. But he always believed that if the Mariners put a winner on the field, more fans would show up.

"Anybody who says it isn't a baseball town, that's baloney," Niehaus said. "I always knew from people I had talked to, the old-timers up here, that this was baseball territory. All you had to do was give the fans here a product they could be proud of. I'm not necessarily saying win the division or go to the World Series. Just give them a competitive ballclub and people would come."

When the Mariners joined the American League in 1977, Niehaus thought they would be a .500 team within five years and the fans would follow.

It took 15 years for the Mariners to win more games than they lost, and the arrival of young stars such as Alvin Davis, Mark Langston, Harold Reynolds, Omar Vizquel, Ken Griffey Jr., Edgar Martinez, and Randy Johnson sparked unparalleled interest in the team in the mid- and late 1980s.

But it wasn't until 1995, in the "Refuse to Lose" season, that the city truly embraced Major League Baseball.

Huge crowds turned the Kingdome, which seemed for years like the worst place to play a baseball game, into a noise chamber. The Mariners fed off it, making up 11½ games in the standings between August 23 and the end of the season to catch the Angels.

When Randy Johnson struck out Tim Salmon for the final out of the tiebreaker playoff on October 2, 1995—26 years to the day that the Pilots played their final game—the celebration was wild.

Those inside the Kingdome not only heard it, they felt it.

"The press box floor moved," said Tim Hevly, then the assistant public relations director. "The building was literally shaking."

It continued through the Mariners' playoff series against the Yankees, which Edgar Martinez won with his dramatic 11th-inning double in Game 5. The magical season ended when Mariners fell in six games to the Cleveland Indians in the American League Championship Series.

As the dust settled in the weeks that followed, the Mariners' office staff began to realize what 1995 meant. The thirst for baseball around the city remained strong even after it all had ended.

At the team's offices near the Kingdome, gifts arrived almost daily.

"It seemed like everybody in town sent something to us," Hevly said. "There were gift baskets and food, and every time we turned around there was something new with a note saying, 'Thanks so much for what you've done for the city.'"

Yes, everyone could finally say Seattle was indeed a baseball town.

"I never thought that this wasn't a baseball town," Julio Cruz said. "I was hoping the team would never move because if they moved, then I'd have to move also, and I didn't want to leave Seattle.

"Every city needs to have baseball. This city is good for baseball and baseball is good for this city."

CHAPTER TWO

A Rocky Beginning

MANAGER DARRELL JOHNSON AND HIS COACHES arrived early for spring training in 1977 and discovered that it would take a lot more work than they thought to begin the Mariners' first camp.

Their task involved the usual pre-camp planning: evaluating personnel, setting the workout regimen, organizing hitting groups and throwing schedules, removing rocks from the infield, filling gopher holes in the outfield.

Wait a minute. Rocks on the infield? Gopher holes in the outfield?

The practice fields at the Mariners' complex in Tempe, Arizona, were in rough shape, and it fell upon Johnson and some of his coaches—the staff consisted of Jim Busby, Don "Bear" Bryant, Wes Stock, and Vada Pinson—to do a large amount of the work to get them in shape.

"They were out there sweating with rakes, trying to get the fields prepared for the arrival of the ballplayers," play-by-play announcer Dave Niehaus said. "The fields hadn't been used in years, and those guys were out there picking boulders off the skin portion of the infield."

Also, the outfield didn't have a warning track, and it was a pot-holed magnet for sprained ankles.

"There were gopher holes in the outfield," pitcher Gary Wheelock said. "The main stadium field wasn't too bad, but the practice fields were in pretty bad shape. The first day we worked out, there were tumbleweeds that had blown onto the fields."

There was more. The Mariners' pitchers, as maligned as they were in those days, literally couldn't have thrown the ball straight had catcher Bob Stinson not made an important discovery. Stinson, having arrived early himself, crouched behind home plate and noticed that the pitcher's mound was off-center, about six inches closer to first base than it was to third base.

Even in the lousiest conditions, there's a magic to spring training. There's a sense of anticipation for even the bad teams, because it's a time when everybody is tied for first place and anything is possible.

That romantic interlude has applied to scores of lousy teams in major-league history...but not the 1977 Mariners.

They knew who they were—mostly castoffs from other teams made available in the expansion draft, veterans in their final years and young prospects getting their first taste of the major leagues.

"An expansion team just didn't get anything in terms of players," pitching coach Wes Stock said. "We ended up with a bunch of old guys who couldn't play or a bunch of young kids who weren't ready. All of us knew what we had and what our job was ahead of us. As coaches, it was just a matter of keeping ourselves up emotionally because we had to keep the players up. If we had given up, then the players would have given up. But you certainly didn't go into it thinking you would win the pennant."

The original Mariners included Dave Collins, a fast young outfielder known in his hometown as the "Rapid City Rabbit," who had played two seasons with the Angels before the Mariners got him in the expansion draft; second baseman Jose Baez, a rookie who lost his job to speedy 22-year-old Julio Cruz at midseason; left fielder Steve Braun, an established veteran with the Twins who played 15 seasons in the majors, but less than one with the Mariners before they traded him to Kansas City in 1978; right fielder Lee Stanton, who was near the end of his nine-year career; third baseman Bill Stein, who played 14 seasons with the Cardinals, White Sox, Mariners, and Rangers; first baseman Dan Meyer, who spent five years with the Mariners before they traded him to Oakland after the 1981 season; center fielder Ruppert Jones, a flashy young player who became the Mariners' first All-Star that season; catcher Bob

Stinson, a tell-it-like-it-is veteran who played four seasons in Seattle to finish a 12-year career; and shortstop Craig Reynolds, a promising young player who had his best years with the Astros after the Mariners traded him in 1978 for pitcher Floyd Bannister.

Veteran right-hander Diego Segui, who had pitched for the Seattle Pilots in 1969, became the Mariners' opening-night starter in '77. Glenn Abbott, Dick Pole, Gary Wheelock, and John Montague got a majority of the starts, although the Mariners essentially were an evolving—and revolving—staff that used 17 different starting pitchers that season.

The Right Man for the Job

The man charged with pulling those young and old players together was manager Darrell Johnson. Mariners general manager Lou Gorman hired Johnson, a former catcher, because of his reputation as an old-school baseball man and disciplinarian, but also for his patience.

Johnson had managed the Red Sox to the American League pennant and the memorable 1975 World Series, which they lost in seven games to the Cincinnati Reds. The Sox, though, wobbled below .500 much of the 1976 season, and Johnson was fired after 86 games. Gorman hired him to lead his expansion Mariners, and Johnson brought a background of success and an image as a hard-nosed intimidator.

"I didn't really know who Darrell Johnson was," said Julio Cruz, then a 22-year-old second baseman. "I remember seeing him in the '75 World Series, and when the cameras would zoom in on him in the dugout, I thought of him as a grouchy-looking man."

The Mariners soon learned that Johnson wasn't the unyielding taskmaster they had envisioned. At spring training, he was patient. He was a teacher. He cared about his players.

"He had just come off arguably the greatest World Series ever played in '75 between the Red Sox and the Reds. He had gone from the penthouse to the crapper to come here," Mariners broadcaster Dave Niehaus said. "But he was an awfully patient guy and he was the right man for the job at the time. He was a hard worker. He was very good to those young players and he cared about them."

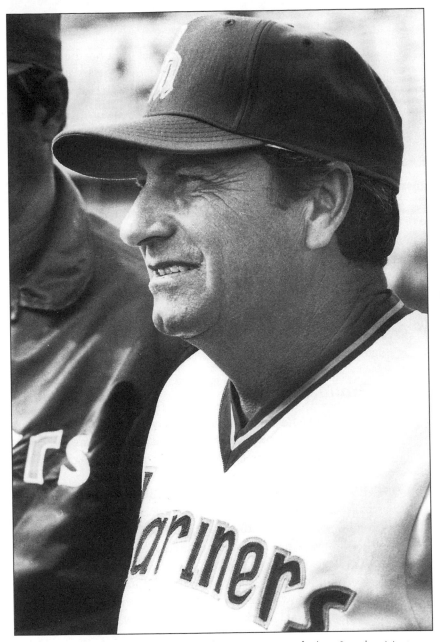

Darrell Johnson was named the first manager of the Seattle Mariners.
Photo courtesy of the Seattle Mariners

It's not that Johnson was all smiles and pats on the back. He occasionally would lay into a player, but he'd do it for all the right reasons. Mostly, he treated the Mariners in a way that would help them improve.

"He was a hard-nosed guy and there were times when he would yell at me," Cruz said. "But he told me up front, 'If I stop yelling at you, that's when you worry. If I yell at you, that means I know you have talent and you can play this game.'"

Pitching coach Wes Stock said anyone who believed that Johnson was overly rough, impatient, and intimidating had based that opinion on reputation, not on how he handled the young Mariners. That's how he's remembered in Seattle.

Twenty-seven years after Johnson took those fledgling Mariners for what became an adventurous three-and-a-half-year run as their manager, he died of leukemia on May 3, 2004, at age 75.

"When he took the job with the Mariners, he knew we were all young and fragile and if he threw out any bad vibes toward us, we might all crawl into a shell," Cruz said. "I loved the man."

A Grand Opening

The 57,762 who packed the Kingdome on April 6, 1977, weren't there just to see a victory, and that turned out to be a good thing. California Angels pitcher Frank Tanana shut out the Mariners 7-0 in the first game in franchise history.

The big picture was what mattered, and Seattle was thrilled that baseball had returned after the bad experience with the Pilots. For one night, the fans loved the Mariners win or lose.

"I will always remember the excitement the town had for the return of baseball," Niehaus said.

Before the opening game, the city honored the team with a parade through downtown and, even though the weather was gray and the players rode open convertibles, there was warmth from all the fans lining the streets.

"It was colder than heck and it was a miserable day," Niehaus said. "But there were people lined up Fourth Avenue welcoming baseball back after that terrible memory of the Pilots in 1969."

The good feelings continued in the Kingdome, where U.S. Senator Henry "Scoop" Jackson of Everett threw out the ceremonial first pitch from a box near the Mariners' third-base dugout. Alongside were commissioner Bowie Kuhn and the Mariners' owners, including entertainer Danny Kaye.

"It was a proud moment," Niehaus said. "They all had such a wonderful time."

Right-hander Diego Segui, who pitched for the Seattle Pilots eight years earlier, threw a strike to Jerry Remy with the first pitch in Mariners history. Then, beginning a tradition followed by Mariners pitchers to this day, Segui issued a leadoff walk.

In the bottom of the first inning, Dave Collins became the first batter in Mariners history, and he set a tone for other Seattle hitters over the years. He took a called third strike from Tanana.

The Angels scored runs in each of the first five innings, including the first Kingdome home run by Joe Rudi in the third, and Tanana pitched a nine-hit complete game to shut out the Mariners 7-0.

"The score was incidental and it didn't make a difference who won that ballgame," Niehaus said. "Major League Baseball was back in the Pacific Northwest, and I was happy to be a part of it. Everybody went home happy even though we got shut out. There was a buzz in the town about baseball and we looked forward to the next game."

"Unfortunately," Niehaus added, "reality set in."

What the Mariners faced the next night may have been worse than reality. Nolan Ryan threw his blazing fastball down their throats in a three-hit complete game—and another shutout, 2-0.

"I was beginning to wonder not only if we were going to win a game, but if we would ever score a run," Niehaus said.

The Mariners did both in their third game.

They scored twice in the bottom of the ninth off Angels reliever John Verhoeven when Bob Stinson and Larry Milbourne hit RBI doubles in a 7-6 comeback victory. It made left-handed reliever Bill Laxton the Mariners' first winning pitcher.

Gary Wheelock, making his first major-league start, held the Angels to four hits in six innings of the fourth game of the five-game series, and Ed Montague pitched two scoreless innings for the save in a 5-1 victory that pulled the Mariners' record to .500.

"I didn't have a very good spring training that year and I was nervous for my first major-league start," Wheelock said.

Angels manager Norm Sherry watched in disbelief as Wheelock, who had come up in the California system before the Mariners took him in the expansion draft, beat his team.

"I remember Norm saying, 'The guy couldn't get anybody out in spring training, and now he comes out and beats us here,'" Wheelock said.

The Mariners' winning ways didn't last long. They lost the next three games and never reached .500 again that year.

Rupe and Cruzer, the First Fan Favorites

Julio Cruz and Ruppert Jones have a standard greeting when they get together for old-timers' functions.

"Rupe, thanks for taking all those pitches for me so I could steal bases," Cruz tells him.

"That's OK, Cruzer," Jones replies, "because I always knew I would get fastballs to hit."

The Mariners didn't win over their fans with victories that first season, but they did produce a few players who became favorites. Two of the most popular were Jones and Cruz, a couple of rookies who brought enthusiasm and speed to the ballpark every day.

Jones had been the No. 1 pick in the expansion draft, but he came to the Mariners with just 51 major-league at-bats the previous season with Kansas City and absolutely no identity among Seattle fans.

That changed quickly.

Jones patrolled center field at the Kingdome with a flare that foreshadowed the amazing feats of Ken Griffey Jr. a dozen years later. Jones became the Mariners' first All-Star in 1977 and played two more years in Seattle before the M's traded him to New York.

The '77 season in Seattle was special, simply because Jones had become so popular with the fans. They loved his name, and every time he would come to bat or make a big play, chants of "Ruuuuuupe! Ruuuuuupe!" would echo through the Kingdome. During the seventh-inning stretch, when fans would sing "Take Me

Ruppert Jones. *Photo courtesy of the Seattle Mariners*

Out to the Ballgame," they altered the words in order to "Rupe, Rupe, Rupe for the home team."

"Everybody got energized because of the name," broadcaster Dave Niehaus said. "Ruppert was the first guy to capture the imagination of Pacific Northwest fans. He had a little flash to him and he had some swagger when he went out to center field. He had a little power and a good arm. He was not a superstar by any stretch of the imagination, but he was our superstar."

Jones hit a career-high 24 home runs that season and drove in 76. After Cruz was called up in July, they complemented each other in the lineup.

"Rupe was a big reason I stole so many bases, because he would take a pitch for me," said Cruz, who stole 15 bases his first season, then 59 in 1978 to rank second in the American League. Cruz was the Mariners' leadoff hitter, and Jones batted either fourth or fifth, and when Cruz reached base, he had a signal for Jones to indicate when he would run.

"I would put a finger in my ear hole, and that meant I would go on that pitch," Cruz said. "He would take the pitch or fake a bunt, just to give me that little edge. But it gave him a little edge, too, because the other teams all knew I was going to run and they would throw him fastballs."

Cruz had spent the first half of the 1977 season tearing up the Pacific Coast League for the Mariners' Class-AAA Calgary team, hitting .374 with 40 steals and 74 runs. The Cannons played a game in Phoenix on July 3 when the equipment manager tipped off Cruz that he was headed to the major leagues.

"He said, 'Cruzer, they're going to call you up tomorrow,'" Cruz said. "I was having a big year and I was thinking, 'Why would they want to call me up? Just let me keep playing here.'"

The next morning, Cruz flew to Seattle and got his first glimpse of the Kingdome as he rode toward downtown from Sea-Tac Airport.

"I saw it from the taxi, and my first thought was, 'What is that? It looks like a flying saucer,'" he said. "Then I thought, 'Geez, I'm going to be playing there.'"

Tired from the trip to Seattle and from answering reporters' calls after he checked into his hotel, Cruz figured he could relax a little when he got to the ballpark. Surely, Cruz thought, he wouldn't be playing that night.

He arrived at the Kingdome and pulled on the knit Mariners uniform—wearing No. 6 in honor of his favorite major leaguer, former Cardinals great Stan Musial—and anticipated a night on the bench to unwind from the whirlwind previous 24 hours.

Didn't happen. The Mariners hadn't called Cruz up to sit him.

Julio Cruz steals third base. *Photo by The Herald of Everett, WA*

"I looked up at the lineup and I was in there," he said. "I was the leadoff guy."

Facing right-hander Francisco Barrios of the White Sox, Cruz flew out to center field in his first at-bat, but singled to center in the fourth inning for his first major-league hit.

As much as his big-league dream came true that night, Cruz relived another that season, on August 30 in New York, when the Mariners played in Yankee Stadium. It was a homecoming for Cruz, who was born in Brooklyn and lived there until his family moved to California when he was 14.

"I remember the day we left, we passed by Yankee Stadium and I said to myself, 'The next time I come to New York, I'm going to play in that stadium,'" Cruz said. Eight years later, he returned as a major leaguer with the Mariners.

"I stood in the same batter's box where Lou Gehrig stood," he said. "I used the same shower that Babe Ruth used. It was such an exuberant feeling. I went early to the ballpark, knowing I was going to play that night in front of my people, in front of my relatives."

Cruz played 60 games for the Mariners that season, batting .256 and stealing 15 bases. In 1978, his first full season, he became one of the American League's top base-stealers. He finished second in the league with 59, including a record 32 straight without being thrown out.

Cruz became a quality defensive player at second base, where Hall of Famer Bill Mazeroski, one of the best defensive second basemen of all time, helped hone his game while on the coaching staff in 1979 and 1980.

On June 7, 1981, less than a week before the players strike shut down baseball for two months, Cruz played one of his greatest games. He handled 18 total chances without an error in nine innings, setting an American League record for second basemen. When the game went 11 innings, he handled one more chance and came up one short of the major-league record.

Cruz made his final statement in that game with his legs. With one out in the bottom of the 11th and the score tied 4-4, he singled off Mike Stanton, then stole second base. Tom Paciorek singled to center with one out, and Cruz sped home with the winning run.

Unfortunately, any joy by the Mariners in those days was an occasional thing, and the losses were hard on Cruz, as they were on the whole team. He endured not only the 98-loss season in the Mariners' first year, but also two others with 100 or more losses.

"We just didn't have the talent to compete at that level, and we knew it going in," he said. "But we had to play the schedule out. It was tough, but personally, I enjoyed every minute I was able to be on the field. I celebrated the fact that I was playing the game of baseball. If I had thought just about wins and losses, I would have gone crazy."

CHAPTER THREE

Lowlights, Highlights, and a Cast of Characters

MARINERS FANS LEARNED NOT TO EXPECT MUCH from their team in the early years, and the M's didn't provide a lot with the hodgepodge of young and old players they threw onto the field. They lost 297 games their first three seasons, and their accomplishments became as much fodder for folklore as anything to brag about.

Take the Mendoza Line. Please take it, Mario Mendoza would say.

Mendoza, a good-fielding, light-hitting shortstop who the Mariners acquired in a trade with the Pirates before the 1979 season, wore the franchise's first label of futility. As his batting average lingered around the .200 mark that season, it became known as the "Mendoza Line"—that statistical barrier separating a poor hitter from a putrid one.

George Brett of the Royals made the term popular, once saying after he'd scanned the batting averages in the newspaper, "I knew I was off to a bad start when I saw my average listed below the Mendoza Line."

A couple of Mendoza's teammates with the Mariners, Tom Paciorek and Bruce Bochte, also are credited with using the term during interviews in 1979, and in later years TV broadcaster Chris Berman brought it into everyone's living rooms with constant references to the Mendoza Line on ESPN.

Whatever the origin, it's Mario Mendoza, the former Mariner, who has been stuck with the label since 1979, when he batted .198 in 148 games. He and Steve Jeltz are the only players to have batted less than .200 while playing at least 148 games. Jeltz, an infielder with the Phillies, batted .187 in 1988.

What's nearly forgotten about Mario Mendoza is the role he played so skillfully in preventing Brett from batting .400 in 1980. After a slow start to the season, Brett's average topped .400 on August 17, and he was batting .394 when the Royals began a late-September trip to the West Coast, beginning with three games at Seattle. Easy pickings, right?

Brett stung the ball throughout that series but was robbed of hits several times on spectacular plays by Mendoza. Brett wound up with just two hits in 11 at-bats through three games at the Kingdome, and when he left Seattle the average had fallen to .389. His run at .400 had suffered a big blow, and he said Mendoza was the reason.

"I still think I should have hit .400 that season," Brett told Jim Street of mlb.com during a 1995 interview. "The reason I didn't was Mario Mendoza. Mendoza took three hits away from me, all right up the middle, on unbelievable plays. I needed five more hits for .400.

"To this day, I hate the sucker," Brett added, joking.

Back-to-Back Thrillers

There wasn't a finer weekend in the early years than a two-day stretch in May 1981, when Tom Paciorek delivered a couple of the sweetest swings in the Mariners' early history.

Paciorek, a 34-year-old outfielder signed by the Mariners in 1978 after he'd been released by the Braves, started the '81 season on a hot streak, batting .377 after three weeks. He'd cooled somewhat by the first of May, but still posed an offensive threat.

May 8 and 9, he showed it.

On a Friday night at the Kingdome, he led off the bottom of the ninth inning of a tie game against the Yankees and homered off Rudy May, giving the Mariners a 3-2 victory.

The next night, May 9, the Mariners trailed 5-3 when Paciorek batted in the ninth again with two outs and two runners on base.

This time he hammered a pitch from Ron Davis for a three-run homer that gave the Mariners a 6-5 victory and set off a wild celebration among the 51,903 fans.

"Those were games you'll never forget if you were a fan back then," play-by-play announcer Dave Niehaus said. "When he hit that home run off Ron Davis, everyone in the Kingdome went crazy."

Armed with baseball bats given away on Bat Night, the crowd clanged their gifts off the metal bleachers during the game, and they continued to use them in the delirium after Paciorek's winning homer.

John McDonald, who covered the Mariners for the *Everett Herald*, had hurried from the press box to the Mariners' clubhouse to get a few quotes from Paciorek. He and everyone else in the clubhouse were astounded at the rumbling they heard from above.

"Everyone was still in the stands and they were banging their bats on the cement," McDonald said. "It sounded like the place was coming apart out there, and it wasn't stopping. Paciorek finally went back out for a curtain call, and that's what it took before everyone stopped banging those bats."

But Can They Play in Vegas?

The Mariners suffered through a meager existence in terms of success, although any joy they couldn't find on the field, they certainly seemed to discover off it. From 1979-83, the Mariners had such fun-loving players as Tom Paciorek, Joe Simpson, Bob Stinson, Larry Andersen and, the master of them all, Bill Caudill.

"We had characters on those early teams, we didn't have players," second baseman Julio Cruz said. "We had funny guys. Some were good players who were funny. Others were just funny."

Bob "Scrap Iron" Stinson was an outspoken veteran catcher obtained from the Royals in the expansion draft, and his candid nature got him in trouble with manager Darrell Johnson right away in 1977. Asked by a newspaper reporter during the team's first spring training when he thought the fledgling Mariners would be eliminated from the division race, Stinson answered honestly.

"Opening Day," he said.

Johnson called Stinson into his office and chewed him out for making that statement, but not because Johnson disagreed. He simply didn't want the Mariners' fans to hear that kind of negative talk before they had a chance to get their hopes up for the new season.

Later in the season, during a game at Milwaukee, Mariners pitcher Glenn Abbott was getting knocked around in the bottom of the first inning after the M's had given him a lead. Pitching coach Wes Stock visited the mound and directed his first question at Stinson.

"What kind of stuff does he have?" Stock asked.

"I can't tell you," Stinson said. "I haven't caught any of his pitches yet."

Back in the dugout, Stock relayed those words to Johnson, who was waiting when Stinson came off the field after the inning. He told his catcher that if he wanted to be a comedian, he should try Las Vegas.

Always Room for JELL-O

The '77 team had its share of fun as the losses—and occasional victories—mounted. "They were just the normal pranks you'd find in any clubhouse," pitcher Gary Wheelock said. "It was stuff like the three-man lift."

Otherwise, that first team was fairly benign compared with the hi-jinx of later years. The king of the early pranks was the Mr. JELL-O Mystery of 1982.

Larry Andersen, a right-handed pitcher on the 1981-82 teams, conspired with teammates Richie Zisk and Joe Simpson on a prank against manager Rene Lachemann, who was a character himself. Lachemann, for example, spent several nights in the Mariners' clubhouse in the Kingdome, figuring it had everything he needed— cable TV, food, a comfortable couch—even though it exposed him to occasional pranks from his players.

No prank gained as much notoriety as what Andersen, Zisk and Simpson pulled on Lachemann on a road trip. After the team landed in Chicago, the three players went to a grocery store and bought 16 boxes of cherry JELL-O, then talked traveling secretary Lee Pelekoudas into giving them the key to Lachemann's hotel room.

They poured several boxes of JELL-O into the toilet, bathtub and sink, then mixed it with a bucket of ice to allow the JELL-O to solidify. That wasn't all of it. They took every piece of the furniture from the room—beds, mattresses, tables and chairs—and crammed them in the bathroom. Then they removed all the light bulbs from the fixtures, took the mouthpiece from the telephone, unplugged the clock and strung toilet paper around the empty room.

"Anything we could think of, we did," Andersen said in a 2001 interview with astrosdaily.com, a website covering the Houston Astros, where he played in the late 1980s. "He came back from a night out and poof, his room was no longer a room."

Lachemann later praised the creativity of the prank, but not before he threatened to call the authorities and have the players fingerprinted and subjected to lie detector tests. Lachemann never followed through to that extent, even though the Mr. JELL-O Mystery continued to have twists and turns the next few months.

Play-by-play announcer Dave Niehaus took part in the shenanigans by telling Lachemann that he had gotten a confession on tape from those responsible. The problem, Niehaus told Lachemann, was that he accidentally erased the tape.

Andersen had a fake newspaper page printed with the headline, "Jello-gate tapes lost, Lach baffled."

"Every place we went the rest of that season, there was JELL-O," Lachemann said. "I had a meeting after a game one day with my coaches, Dave Duncan and Bill Plummer. We'd usually have a beer when we got together like that. Those two took one drink of their beer and then spit the stuff out. It turned out someone has gotten into our cans of beer and figured a way to pour out all the beer and replace it with JELL-O.

"It was amazing."

Lachemann had become convinced that an accessory to the crime was outfielder Tom Paciorek, a former fun-loving Mariner who played that year for the White Sox. Because the prank occurred in Chicago, it seemed likely that Paciorek could have been involved. He wasn't, but when the prank gained national attention and

Paciorek's name was linked with other suspects, his mother called Lachemann to apologize for the actions of her son.

The pranksters didn't reveal themselves until the Mariners held their season-ending party. Andersen, Simpson and Zisk appeared with their heads covered by bags that were made to look like JELL-O boxes and taunted Lachemann a final time with a game of "What's My Line."

"In all the years I've been in the game, that's the best prank I've ever seen," Lachemann said in 2006. "It was a great, great prank and it went on the whole year."

Bill Caudill and His Bag of Tricks

Right-handed pitcher Bill Caudill brought legitimacy to the Mariners' bullpen when he arrived in a trade with the Yankees just before the 1982 season. He also had a Sherlock Holmes cap, a pair of handcuffs and a zaniness that helped keep the Mariners' spirits up when the season went south.

The Mariners fielded their first reasonably competitive (remember, that's a relative term when talking about the early Mariners) team in 1982, and Caudill was a big part of it. Not only did he finish fourth in the American League with 26 saves, he also finished with 21 decisions, going 12-9.

"He threw hard, 98 miles an hour, and when we needed a save, we went to him," second baseman Julio Cruz said.

The high point was July 8, when Caudill recorded his 17th save in a 4-3 victory over the Orioles at the Kingdome, pulling the Mariners seven games over .500 at 45-38 and leaving them just three games behind first-place Kansas City in the American League West.

"He was great in the clubhouse, but the main thing is that he was an outstanding pitcher," manager Rene Lachemann said.

Good times on the field, of course, didn't last. These were the Mariners, after all.

They lost seven of their next eight and fell from contention. As important as Caudill was on the mound during the Mariners' successes, he played just as big a role, maybe bigger, off the mound when the team needed an emotional boost during hard times.

Bill Caudill. *Photo courtesy of the Seattle Mariners*

Caudill was a cutup around the clubhouse, and the only times anything or anyone were truly safe from his antics were when he was on the mound.

It started early in the season after the Mariners had lost seven of their first nine games. Caudill got hold of a Sherlock Holmes-style houndstooth cap and conducted an inspection of the Mariners' bats as he searched for the missing hits responsible for such a poor start.

Teammates began calling Caudill "The Inspector"—as in Inspector Clouseau of the "Pink Panther"—and a persona was born.

Dick Kimball, the Kingdome organist, fed Caudill's new image by playing the "Pink Panther" theme when he entered games, and the fans got into it. They would send Caudill all sorts of items, and his box of goodies included an inspector's badge, magnifying glasses, a couple of stuffed pink panthers and a Calabash pipe.

Caudill used those props to play pranks on teammates and others brave enough to venture near him before and after games. He also tried some unconventional tricks when everything else failed to shake the Mariners out of their losing ways.

One night, after being called out of the bullpen to pitch a tight game against the Blue Jays in 1983, Caudill appeared with half a beard, talked into it by a teammate, pitcher Roy Thomas.

In the opposing dugout, Barry Bonnell told his Blue Jays teammates that he would knock the other half of the beard off Caudill's face when he came to bat. Bonnell nearly did, blistering a line drive off Caudill's chest that deflected to second baseman Tony Bernazard, who threw out Bonnell at first base. Caudill ducked into the clubhouse after that inning and shaved off the rest of the beard, then pitched a scoreless ninth.

Caudill did his greatest damage with a pair of handcuffs he acquired as a memento of a misadventure during a road series in Cleveland. He'd been in the lobby at the team hotel well past midnight after the team had arrived from New York. Security guards, wary of anyone lingering around the hotel at that time of day because of a series of car thefts in the vicinity, stopped Caudill and questioned him. Caudill's answers apparently didn't satisfy the security guards, who slapped a pair of handcuffs on him and threatened to call police. Word of the incident got upstairs to Lachemann, who reported to the lobby and talked the guards into letting him deal with Caudill.

Lachemann guided Caudill to his room and the incident was over. Or so he thought.

Mariners designated hitter Richie Zisk made sure the residue of that night remained forever, giving Caudill a pair of handcuffs.

Caudill didn't simply keep them around as a symbol of his episode in Cleveland, he put them to constant use.

When Caudill wasn't slapping those cuffs on an unsuspecting victim, he had everyone else wary of them. Soon, "The Inspector" acquired a second nickname: "Cuffs."

Before one game, Caudill had an idea for Lachemann.

"When you call me down in the bullpen, give me the 'cuffs' sign," Caudill told his manager, holding up his wrists as if they were clasped together.

Later that night, when Lachemann needed Caudill to warm up, he flashed the "cuffs" sign. Caudill got loose and Lachemann brought him into the game.

"Then he gave up a three-run homer and blew the save," Lachemann said. "We put that 'cuffs' sign on the back burner after that."

The handcuffs became a common sight at the ballpark, home and away.

"He always had them with him, and he would walk up to you and just slap them on you," Cruz said. "Or he would come up and say, 'Let me see if these will fit,' and cuff you, and then walk away. That's how he got the owner's wife."

Judie Argyros, wife of owner George Argyros, was in the Mariners dugout before a game at the Kingdome when Caudill demonstrated his handcuffs. He clasped one cuff on her wrist, the other to the dugout bench, and walked away. She remained stranded while players warmed up for the game, while the grounds crew prepared the field and while everyone else stood at attention during the National Anthem.

Just before the first pitch, Caudill freed her.

Caudill never got those cuffs onto George Argyros, although he did pull a good one on the owner during contract negotiations with the Mariners. Caudill was represented by a budding young agent named Scott Boras, who was Caudill's roommate when they played minor-league baseball together. Boras got Argyros to agree on a contract clause that allowed Caudill to throw a dozen balls into the crowd at each game.

That was no small feat back then, because Argyros maintained strict control of expenses. He would station an employee in the press box to monitor players who threw baseballs into the crowd, and those who did would have the price of the balls deducted from their pay. All except Caudill, that is.

Larry Andersen, a pitcher on the 1981 and '82, teams, often was a partner in Caudill's playfulness. Andersen had a Conehead mask—made famous by the old *Saturday Night Live* characters—that he kept throughout his major-league travels, and Caudill plucked it from his locker during a rain delay in Detroit. He pulled the Conehead over his head, stuffed his jersey so it was nice and plump, then entertained the crowd with an animated parody of fellow pitcher Gaylord Perry, complete with a mimicking of Perry's reputed doctoring of the baseball.

Perry was so agitated he tried to tear off the cone…with Caudill's head still in it.

CHAPTER FOUR

Travel Travails

IT DIDN'T TAKE LONG FOR THE MARINERS TO LEARN one difficult lesson about playing baseball in the Northwest corner of the country. Seattle isn't close to anywhere, especially if the destination is another major-league city.

Before the Mariners finished first in any meaningful baseball statistic, they led the league in mileage.

They fly about 50,000 miles a year and, unlike the convenience and relative privacy of the chartered flights that today's team uses, the early Mariners almost always flew commercial.

Former owner George Argyros mandated it in order to save money, which it did. But traveling that way became horribly inconvenient, and the Mariners' itinerary was dictated largely by airline schedules. They traveled numerous times on off days, and flying commercial meant they often had to take connecting flights that extended their travel time between cities.

Flying commercial also forced the players to mix with the paying customers on flights, which made for some interesting moments. On most trips, the Mariners would fly bigger jets with enough first-class seats for the entire team, separating the ballplayers from the other passengers.

"But a lot of times, especially when we would be connecting, we would stop in a city like Chicago and change planes, and we would take a smaller plane for the next leg of a trip," said Lee Pelekoudas, the traveling secretary. "Then we'd have 12 first-class seats and the rest of the guys would be sitting in the coach section. There would be some interesting interaction with the public, some positive, some negative."

Frank Howard's Pre-Flight "Announcement"

Frank Howard, the Mariners hitting coach in 1988, decided to use his new headphones to listen to music during a flight to Southern California. The Mariners had climbed aboard an AirCal jet, an older DC-9 that was configured with three seats on one side of the aisle and two on the other. The team would use most of the three-seat side of the plane, leaving the other side for the general public.

Lee Pelekoudas sat in one row, and behind him were Howard and pitching coach Billy Connors, with clubhouse worker Pete Fortune in the middle seat between them.

"Frank had gotten some headphones to listen to music, but he'd never worn headphones before," Pelekoudas said. "Frank had a loud, booming voice anyway, and with the headphones on and the music playing, it made him talk even louder without realizing it."

Just before takeoff, just as everyone became quiet, a thought crossed Howard's mind and he shared it with Connors. Plus just about everyone else on that flight.

"Hey Billy!" Howard said, that deep voice carrying throughout the jet. "How 'bout when we get back to Seattle after this trip, we hit the town and…"

Let's just say they weren't going grocery shopping.

"He said it so loud that the whole plane heard it," Pelekoudas said. "I remember my head popping up and I was thinking, 'Oh no, this isn't happening.'"

It was.

Pelekoudas looked across the aisle to see an elderly woman's jaw drop. Pete Fortune, sitting between Howard and Connors, looked across the aisle in his row to see a mother and her young son. She was covering the boy's ears.

Howard, of course, had no idea he'd offended anyone.

"Frank was having a good old time," Pelekoudas said. "It didn't dawn on him what was going on until he took his headphones off and we told him."

Howard felt horrible and apologized.

"Well, I'm sorry ma'am," he told the elderly woman.

"Frank was a very polite guy and he was very apologetic afterwards," Pelekoudas said. "That was one of the dangers of traveling commercial."

Gaylord Perry's Flight to 300

The Mariners were in the middle of an East Coast trip early in the 1982 season when pitcher Gaylord Perry beat the Yankees in New York for his 299th career victory.

After that April 30 game, the team traveled by bus to Baltimore to finish the trip, then planned to fly back to Seattle—commercial, as usual—on an off day before they began a home series against the Yankees. Perry was scheduled to pitch the opener against New York.

But on the day he pitched in New York, Perry told Pelekoudas, "If I win 299 tonight, we're chartering home."

Perry's idea was to fly immediately after the final game in Baltimore so the players could spend their day off at home in Seattle instead of traveling.

"That's fine, if you can work it out," Pelekoudas told Perry.

That meant flying the idea past team owner George Argyros, who was a brick wall to almost any idea that involved spending more money.

"By the time the bus got down to Baltimore and I walked into my hotel room, the phone was ringing," Pelekoudas said. "It was George, and he proceeded to scream at me for probably 15 minutes."

Argyros was livid. "Don't you ever give my phone number out again. We're not going to charter," he told Pelekoudas.

"George, I didn't give anyone your phone number," Pelekoudas said.

Didn't matter. Perry had gotten Argyros' number and already had run the idea past the owner, and the big guy didn't like it.

Later, Argyros called Pelekoudas back and apologized for getting upset, and they had a long discussion about team travel. Pelekoudas explained why it was best for the players that they didn't spend an entire off day flying back home, and in this case he'd like to grant Perry his wish.

"OK, you can get a charter," Argyros told Pelekoudas, adding one difficult provision, "as long as it doesn't cost any more than a commercial flight."

Faced with a situation almost as difficult as hitting a grand slam with two men on base, Pelekoudas jumped on the phone. He called a friend with Ozark Airlines and got lucky. Ozark had just flown a military charter from Seattle to the East Coast, and Pelekoudas talked the airline into letting the Mariners use the jet for the return trip.

"I pleaded with them to get the cost down to what the commercial cost would be for us, which was about $19,000 or $20,000," Pelekoudas said.

The airline agreed to it and Pelekoudas called Argyros, who gave his approval.

"Gaylord got his wish," Pelekoudas said.

Two nights later, on May 6 after a day off without travel, Perry beat the Yankees to win his 300th.

Don't Forget the Skipper

On the field, nothing could stop the Mariners during the 2001 season, when they tied the all-time record with 116 victories. Off the field, they had their moments.

The Mariners were playing a mid-June inter-league series in Colorado when Ron Spellecy, the traveling secretary, became ill and underwent quadruple bypass surgery. With Spellecy down for several weeks, the Mariners handed his duties to Jim Fitzgerald, who was a baseball operations assistant under GM Pat Gillick.

"Get on the next plane to Oakland," Lee who had become the assistant general manager, told Fitzgerald. "For the foreseeable future, you're our traveling secretary."

Fitzgerald was the best man for the job, even if he didn't feel like the right man for it.

"Traveling secretary is the hardest job in baseball. I did not know anything about cars, buses, trains, airplanes, hotels," he said. "I flew down there and just pieced it together. I was learning as I was going. I was arranging tickets and on the phone with the hotel people handling all kinds of details. Players were telling me things like, 'My wife is coming in early. I need a crib. I need a connecting room. I need a car.'"

Somehow, Fitzgerald pulled together all those details without a major snafu, and the Mariners made it back from Oakland for a six-game homestand before hitting the road again.

Sunday, June 28, was getaway day, with the Mariners flying to Anaheim after the homestand finale against Oakland. The A's had beaten the Mariners 6-3 and, although the M's remained 18 games ahead of the second-place Angels in the division standings, manager Lou Piniella was angry at having lost.

Meanwhile, Fitzgerald did his best to hustle the players, coaches, and personnel out of the clubhouse and onto the bus for the short drive to Boeing Field, where the Mariners' chartered jet waited to fly them to Anaheim.

"The bus always leaves one hour after the final pitch, and since the game ended at five o'clock, I wrote on the message board that the bus would leave at six," Fitzgerald said.

As six o'clock approached, the clubhouse was nearly vacant as the last of the traveling party was either on the bus or driving on their own to the airport.

"It's about two minutes until six and I'm looking around the clubhouse, and it's empty," Fitzgerald said. "I opened the door to Lou Piniella's office, and it's empty. I say to myself, 'All right, the bus is leaving.'"

Pelekoudas, who had driven his own car to the airport, called Fitzgerald to make sure the bus would depart on time.

"Are you guys leaving?" Pelekoudas asked.

"Yeah, it's six o'clock and the bus is pulling out," Fitzgerald said.

"Do you have Lou?" Pelekoudas asked.

"No, but I checked his office and he wasn't there, so he must be driving on his own," Fitzgerald said.

The bus arrived at the airport and everyone had boarded the jet when Fitzgerald's phone rang again. It was a security officer at Safeco Field.

"Do not leave," he told Fitzgerald. "Lou just walked out of here and there's no bus. One of the batboys is driving him there now."

When Fitzgerald had peeked into Piniella's empty office before boarding the bus, he forgot to check one important place: the shower attached to the office. That's where Piniella was as the bus pulled away without him, and one thought filled Fitzgerald's head.

"I am so fired," he said to himself.

On the plane as the team waited for Piniella, Fitzgerald could hear many of the players cackling in the background, especially center fielder Mike Cameron and right fielder Jay Buhner.

"If you have any guts at all," Buhner told Fitzgerald, "you'd have this plane take off right now."

Wisely, Fitzgerald didn't. He did, however, try to remain inconspicuous in the back of the jet, hoping Piniella would take his seat and not scream too loudly at being left at the ballpark. While they waited for Piniella to arrive, Pelekoudas told Fitzgerald to begin handing out the 30 envelopes containing meal money.

"When you're finished, stay in the back of the plane," Pelekoudas told Fitzgerald. "Because when Lou gets here, he's going to be hot."

Piniella finally arrived, took his seat at the front of the jet and didn't say a word. The jet took off and, after leveling off at about 30,000 feet, Fitzgerald built up enough courage to walk to the front and give Piniella every opportunity to ream him.

"Lou, I'm sorry I left you," Fitzgerald said. "I apologize."

"That's OK kid, don't worry about it," Piniella told him.

The travel tale didn't end there.

Later on that road trip, during a series at Texas, Cameron called for a session of Kangaroo Court, where Fitzgerald faced charges of leaving the manager at Safeco Field. The fine was $10, and Fitzgerald knew that it would double if he fought the charges and lost. Rarely does a defendant convince the usually unyielding Kangaroo Court to overturn a case, but Fitzgerald fought this one with a passionate plea.

"I wrote on the board that the bus was leaving at six o'clock," he told the court. "Well, there's a new sheriff in town! When I say the bus leaves at six o'clock, it leaves at six o'clock!"

That drew a murmur from the players and a protest from Piniella.

"Well, then I'm hanging the sheriff!" Piniella said.

Cameron, swayed by Fitzgerald's speech, delivered his ruling.

"You're right," Cameron said. "Lou, you're fined for being late for the bus. You owe 10 bucks."

"But the kid left me behind!" Piniella pleaded. "He left me!"

Didn't matter, Piniella had to pay up.

For the rest of the 2001 season, even after Spellecy returned to his traveling secretary duties, Fitzgerald was known as "The Sheriff."

CHAPTER FIVE

When All Else Fails, Give Something Away

SEATTLE HAS LONG EMBRACED BIG EVENTS.

The annual unlimited hydroplane boat races would draw hundreds of thousands to Lake Washington. The NCAA played its Final Four in the Kingdome three times, bringing big crowds and Chamber of Commerce notoriety to the city. University of Washington football games drew tailgating crowds to Husky Stadium a half-dozen Saturdays each fall, and the NFL Seahawks filled the Kingdome on Sundays. Even the Mariners made a splash when they hosted the All-Star Game in 1979.

The Mariners' big challenge, however, was trying to sell the everyday concept of baseball.

Opening Day sold out annually, but that was never a true gauge of the interest in baseball. The Mariners' first opening night in 1977 drew 57,762 to the Kingdome; their second game drew 10,144. They drew more than 1.3 million in the first season when the return of baseball became somewhat fashionable, but they didn't come close to breaking one million the next four years.

"In those early years we learned that it was an event town," said Randy Adamack, then the Mariners' public relations director. "Opening Day for us is a big event, and at certain times during the year a Mariners game would have a big focus. Our challenge was that we played 81 times here and we needed to make each one of them an event."

To do that, they did what all good promoters would do when their product alone wasn't enough to fill the seats. They gave stuff away.

The Mariners had hat nights. They had bat nights. They gave away T-shirts and jackets. They also brought in entertainment, some of it good, some lousy, to entice folks into spending beautiful summer Saturday nights inside the concrete dome.

Some of those promotions were big hits, some were flops, and many became part of the Mariners' lore.

Face of the Franchise: Funny Nose Glasses

The Mariners gave jackets to fans during one promotion in 1981, and to publicize the event they put together a TV commercial starring outfielder Tom Paciorek.

His sales pitch: "Hi everybody, I'm Tom Paciorek of the Seattle Mariners. This Saturday night, come to the Kingdome because the first 30,000 fans will receive a pair of these great funny nose glasses. That's right, funny nose glasses."

Paciorek put on a pair of the glasses, featuring a big bulb of a nose and a black mustache, when a voice from behind the camera interrupted.

"No Tom, it's not Funny Nose Glasses Night, it's Jacket Night. The first 30,000 will get a Mariners jacket."

Paciorek looked stunned. "Then what am I supposed to do with 30,000 pairs of funny nose glasses?" he asked.

"Tom," the voice added, "that's your problem."

Jacket Night went over well, as most Saturday night giveaways did, but the commercial starring Paciorek left fans with a taste for more, specifically noses and glasses. The Mariners were besieged with calls from fans wanting a Funny Nose Glasses Night. In 1982, those fans got their wish.

The Mariners scheduled the promotion for May 8 and the response was overwhelming. A crowd of 36,716 showed up, almost 10,000 more than two nights earlier when Gaylord Perry beat the Yankees for his 300th career victory.

Men, women and children wore their funny nose glasses in the stands, owner George Argyros and his wife, Judie, wore them, as did the Mariners themselves. The relief pitchers walked to the bullpen before the game wearing them, all looking like the sons of one really ugly daddy, and manager Rene Lachemann wore a pair to home plate for the pregame meeting with umpires.

Plate umpire Tom Haller took one look at Lachemann and said, "No wonder you guys are in last place."

Hold the Smoke

Randy Adamack had flown into Seattle on July 5, 1978, the day before he began his new job as the Mariners' public relations director. After he got settled in his hotel room, he opened the sports section to get a feel for what was going on with the Mariners.

"There was a story at the bottom of the page saying how the laser light show scheduled for July 4 had been smoked out," he said. Intrigued, he read on.

Immediately after the Mariners lost 5-3 to the A's, the crew responsible for the postgame Fourth of July laser show began setting up its equipment behind second base, in the middle of the Kingdome field. Part of the look was to pump enough smoke into the dome for the lasers to have a cool effect.

"The problem is that they put out about 10 times more smoke into the building than they should have," Adamack said. "The whole place was filled with smoke and they had to evacuate the building. By the time the smoke cleared about an hour and a half later, there wasn't anybody left to see the show."

It did go on, however.

"A handful of people from the staff were still hanging around," Adamack said, "and they said it was a heck of a laser light show."

Mascot Maniacs

The San Diego Chicken had become a phenomenal success in the late 1970s, and the Mariners decided to catch that wave 1981. Not just by having the Chicken show up at their ballpark, but by staging a mascot contest.

They called it the International Mascot Competition and invited anyone interested in being considered as a mascot for the Mariners to come to the Kingdome and perform before a game. More than two dozen showed up.

There was a circus performer from Bulgaria who wore a rabbit costume and called himself the "Bulgarian Rabbit." One guy followed a classic Northwest motif and was a roller-skating salmon. Another wore a white suit, and from the waist up he had concocted a replica of the Seattle Space Needle that was about 10 feet tall.

Then there was a guy who called himself "The Baby." He wore a crewcut, crooked glasses, a diaper that covered just the right places, and nothing else.

Adamack was one of two Mariners employees who served as judges, along with *Seattle Post-Intelligencer* sportswriter J. Michael Kenyon.

"We introduced the mascots individually and they would come out of the left-field gate and make their way across the field, past third base and over to foul territory in front of our dugout," Adamack said. "Then they would wave, do flips, rollerskate, whatever it took to impress the crowd and the judges."

Staying in character, The Baby crawled the entire way on his hands and knees, a distance of about 100 yards over the abrasive artificial turf of the Kingdome.

"When he got to the dugout, he stood up to wave at the crowd, and his hands and his knees were blood red," Adamack said. "He had worn them raw crawling across the field."

One judge voted for the Space Needle and Kenyon favored The Baby. Adamack was mulling his deciding vote when Kenyon leaned over and said, "I'm going to rip you guys in the newspaper if you don't pick The Baby."

Adamack couldn't be swayed. He picked the Space Needle.

"J. Michael didn't talk to me for about a month," Adamack said.

"I don't think that promotion drew an extra fan that night," he added. "But around town it created some talk. It was something that was written about and it was very visual for TV. Our games were on TV only about 20 times all season, and in 1981 we were just happy to have anyone mention our name."

Buhner Buzz: A Cut Above

The crowning glory of the Mariners' promotions, at least in the post-Funny Nose Glasses era, was Buhner Buzz Night. Anyone who showed up bald like Mariners right fielder Jay Buhner got into the game free. For those who didn't arrive hairless, employees from a chain of salons were outside the ballpark with their clippers buzzing, shearing Buhner fans bald in exchange for donations to support breast cancer research.

Seven Buhner Buzz Nights drew 22,302, among them 298 women.

The idea for the promotion sprang in the early 1990s from an on-the-air jab at Buhner's shrinking hairline by Yankees announcer Phil Rizzuto.

"That's a summer haircut," Rizzuto said, pointing out the horseshoe of hair that remained on Buhner's balding noggin. "Summer good and summer bad. That one's really bad."

Jay Buhner is all smiles in the dugout. *Photo by Justin Best/The Herald of Everett, WA*

The Mariners' marketing staff saw that and, during a brainstorm meeting, came up with the Buhner Buzz Night idea. The first one in 1994 drew 512, including two women, who sat in a special bald-only section in the Kingdome behind Buhner's position in right field. The Mariners considered it a success, although that head count was nothing compared with future Buzz Nights.

In 2001, when the final Buzz Night was held one year after Buhner retired, 6,246 participated, including 112 women. Among them was 77-year-old Helyn Nelson, who auctioned off her hair and raised $148 for a group of students at her church to participate in a mission to Fiji.

At every Buzz Night, Buhner would take a break from his pregame duties to join fans at the buzz-cut stations outside the Kingdome—and at Safeco Field for the final one. He often grabbed a pair of clippers and buzzed away himself. Among his clients one year were his two sons, Gunnar and Chase.

The Mariners also flew Buhner's father to Seattle from Texas to surprise his son during one Buzz Night. When Jay came outside to mingle with his fans, Dad was sitting in a barber's chair.

The two embraced, then Jay shaved his dad bald, too.

Class Actors

Nobody would confuse ballplayers with comedic actors, but the Mariners became known since the mid-1990s for the funny commercials that aired each year as part of their ticket sales campaign.

"The team had some modest success in 1993 and we realized that we had some personalities here," said Kevin Martinez, the club's marketing director. "This was kind of uncharted waters because we had never used players as actors. But we really felt like there was a need to foster the bond between the players and the fans. Those of us who are around them every day get to see their sense of humor, and the question we asked was how to bring it out."

The answer, for a series of commercials produced in 1994, was to feature manager Lou Piniella as an impatient psychiatrist, pitcher Randy Johnson as a sometimes-wild circus knife thrower, outfielder

Jay Buhner as a bombing standup comedian and pitcher Chris Bosio as an aggressive dentist.

"That first year," Martinez said, "there was a lot of skepticism among the players."

Bosio, for example, wasn't keen on the first idea thrown to him. The Mariners had wanted the beefy pitcher to dress as a ballerina. He listened to that concept in a meeting with producers, then took the board of sketches and broke it over his knee.

"Guys," Bosio said, "I'm here to help, but I'm not going to be a ballerina."

Producers and the marketing staff regrouped and, the next day, presented a new idea: Bosio as a mean, nasty dentist staring down the throat of a frightened patient, much the way he did with hitters from the mound. He loved it and so did the viewing public. Most of them, at least.

"We got complaints from a lot of dentists," Martinez said.

Buhner's first commercial featured him as an uninspiring standup comedian whose jokes fall flat in a quiet nightclub. "Here's one for you," he began. "Horse walks into a bar. Bartender says, 'Why the long face?'"

The nightclub audience didn't stir, so Buhner went to another joke that also didn't work: "Here's one for you…"

Years later, during a ceremony at Safeco Field to honor Buhner after his retirement, he began his speech with, "Here's one for you …"

Piniella, the fiery manager known for his intolerance for losing and impatience with soft players, became the perfect man to play a psychiatrist. That commercial began with the camera focused on an office door labeled "Dr. Piniella, Psychiatrist." Behind it was the shadow of a hulking figure who had a patient on the couch.

"Whine, whine, whine!" shouted the voice behind the door, obviously Piniella's. "All you do is come in here and whine! Now get off your duff and stop acting like a loser!"

The next scene shows the door opening and Piniella sticking out his head, saying, "Next!"

Johnson, known in the mid-1990s for his blazing fastball and occasional lack of control with it, portrayed a circus knife thrower whose skill drew cheers from the crowd as he "threw" knives toward a pretty young assistant.

The camera remained on Johnson as he made a final throw, and all viewers could hear was a huge gasp by the circus crowd. Johnson, who obviously had missed his spot, shrugged as if to say, "Oh, well, stuff happens."

"A couple of upset people called because they thought Randy killed the girl," Martinez said.

The commercials became as popular with the Mariners as they were with viewers, and despite long sessions in front of the camera, the players rarely complained and nobody became so impatient that they walked out of a taping. One came close, though.

Joey Cora and Alex Rodriguez were taping one commercial that would show what happens on the team plane during a long flight between cities. The kicker to the commercial was a scene showing Cora and Rodriguez being entertained by a puppet show.

"After they did their lines, Joey and Alex had to sit there as we did this silly puppet show," Martinez said. "It was taking quite a while to get things right, and the director said, 'We're going to need a couple more takes.'"

Cora, tired of waiting, looked at Martinez and said, "It's time to go, bro."

"Joey had had enough of the puppet show," Martinez said. "We got two more takes and that was it."

CHAPTER SIX

Dave Niehaus

THE VOICE OF THE FRANCHISE

DAVE NIEHAUS PULLED UP A CHAIR in the KVI radio booth in the Kingdome, opened a notebook and wrote a number one at the top of a clean score sheet. Niehaus, the play-by-play voice of the Mariners since that first game on April 6, 1977, has numbered every score sheet since.

On June 8, 2006, in his 30th season calling Mariners games, he reached 4,500.

"Once I get to 5,000, that's probably when it stops," he said. "I'm not going to say definitely, but probably. It's been a long, long time."

And it's been a ride that made Niehaus not only one of the most popular of all Mariners, but also an icon in the Pacific Northwest.

"This franchise has been so lucky to have somebody like Dave over the years," team president Chuck Armstrong said. "Even in the 1980s, our radio ratings were among the highest in baseball. We attributed it to Dave. He has the unique ability to make you feel like he's your friend. In the fans' minds he is, because he's in their homes 162 times a summer."

Niehaus has been a finalist four times for the famed Ford C. Frick Award for baseball broadcast excellence. He was nominated for the award in 2003, 2004, 2005 and 2006 in a nationwide vote of fans, who made him their top vote-getter in 2005.

Fans know that when Niehaus screams "It will fly away!" a Mariner has hit a home run, and when he shouts "My, oh my!" there's drama on the diamond. Those signature calls, along with thousands of highlights and lowlights with the Mariners, developed out of a love for baseball from his earliest years.

Niehaus grew up in baseball-rich Middle America, in the small southwest Indiana town of Princeton. He got his baseball influence from his father, who was an avid fan of the game and a friend of the Hodge family, whose son Gil would become an eight-time All-Star and manage the 1969 Miracle Mets. ("By the way," Niehaus says. "It's Hodge, not Hodges. A lot of people make that mistake.")

Living in Princeton, about 170 miles from St. Louis, it was difficult to become anything but a Cardinals fan. Niehaus became enthralled with the Redbirds while sitting on his front porch listening to their games on the radio.

"We had a big Zenith in the living room, and after supper we would turn that radio on and turn it up loud, then go out on the front porch and sit on the swing," Niehaus said.

He would listen to Harry Caray, the Cardinals' energetic play-by-play announcer, as he describe a setting that seemed like baseball heaven.

Niehaus' parents, Jack and Delania, took him to Sportsman's Park in St. Louis for the first time when he was about 10. He remembers the ballpark being as pristine as he'd imagined from the radio broadcasts.

"But when the ballplayers came out, it was a letdown," he said. "Harry Caray had made them seem larger than life, but to me they were just like the guys I'd seen at Bosse Field."

Several years earlier, Niehaus had seen his first professional game at Bosse Field, a stately old minor-league stadium—still in existence as the third oldest pro ballpark in America—in Evansville, Indiana. Back then it was home to the Evansville Bees.

Part of Niehaus' baseball education also took place in a pool hall in downtown Princeton. The place was active every night with men shooting pool and baseball scores flowing in through a ticker.

"I can still see the guy up there at the chalkboard with a little glass of water and a piece of chalk," he said. "As the scores would come over the ticker, he would dip the chalk in water and write a zero or a two or whatever the score was. He had very, very neat handwriting, and it would dry real white. I used to sit there and be fascinated with that."

That fascination carried Niehaus through school—he graduated from Indiana University—and into broadcasting. He worked for the Armed Forces radio and TV service, first calling Dodgers games, then the Yankees, plus hockey and basketball in New York. He returned to Los Angeles in the late 1960s to call baseball, basketball, and football games, then joined Dick Enberg and Don Drysdale in 1969 on California Angels broadcasts.

Back in the Saddle, in Seattle

Dave Niehaus pursued the opportunity to become a lead play-by-play voice when the Mariners were granted an expansion franchise for the 1977 season. He got that job and arrived in Seattle just as unknown to the fans as many of the players were.

"I was a raw rookie," he said. "I'd never really spent any time in Seattle. I'd been through Seattle doing UCLA basketball and football, but I didn't know what to expect."

The moments before his first Mariners broadcast—when they played the California Angels at the Kingdome—were nerve-wracking enough, and the presence of Angels owner Gene Autry made it doubly so. Niehaus had worked in Los Angeles for Autry.

"I had a minute or two before we went on the air and I was sitting there concentrating," Niehaus said. "Then I felt a tap on my back. It was The Cowboy."

Autry smiled at Niehaus and said, "David, how are you? Are they treating you all right in Seattle?"

"They're treating me just fine, Gene, just fine," Niehaus responded.

"That's great to hear, David," Autry said. "By the way, is there a place in the whole Kingdome where a man can get a drink?"

Niehaus had become keenly aware over the years that Autry drank vodka in a glass, and he also knew that there was a bar just behind the broadcast booth in the Kingdome.

"What would you like to drink?" Niehaus asked.

Broadcaster Dave Niehaus sits in the empty stands at Safeco Field prior to the start of the game. *Photo by Dan Bates/The Herald of Everett, WA*

"Well, David, just a shot of vodka will do," Autry said. "A big, big shot of vodka."

Niehaus hurried back to the bar, grabbed a big plastic cup and asked the bartender to fill it with vodka. He rushed back to the broadcast booth and gave the cup of vodka to Autry, then tried to compose himself as the radio broadcast began.

"Hello everybody, this is Dave Niehaus with Ken Wilson, and welcome to Mariners baseball," he said on the air. "We'll meet our special guest, manager Darrell Johnson, right after this break."

Niehaus caught his breath again and turned around to see Autry still standing behind him.

"David, I should never have let your ass go," Autry said, before taking his vodka and walking out of the booth.

Niehaus remembers the first Mariners team to be interesting, if not particularly good. Those Mariners rekindled the memory of Niehaus' time in Los Angeles when he listened to Bill Rigney, manager of the first Angels team in 1961, address his players at spring training in Palm Springs.

"They were all a bunch of castoffs who nobody wanted, draft picks from other clubs, 26th and 27th guys," Niehaus said. "When he made his first speech, he told those players, 'Guys, nobody in this game has ever gone 162-0. We've got a shot.'

"I always remembered those words when it came to that first Mariners team."

They weren't very good, but they allowed him to tell a nightly drama that lasted all summer.

Painting a Picture With Words

Dave Niehaus developed a style that Mariners fans came to love. He told stories and described the scene vividly for listeners. That was important in the early days of the franchise because Mariners games rarely were on TV. Only 17 games were televised each of the first two seasons, and no more than 20 until 1982.

It became Niehaus' responsibility to bring the images of the Kingdome to radios throughout the Northwest, just as Harry Caray did when Niehaus was a kid on his front porch in Indiana.

"Dave paints the best word picture of any baseball announcer I've heard," Mariners president Chuck Armstrong said.

And he's best known for his signature phrases.

Niehaus isn't certain when "My, oh my!" joined his repertoire, but it became so effective that the Mariners had it plastered on buses and bumper stickers one season.

"I'd always used it and I don't know where it came from," Niehaus said. "But what else is there to say? It seems so natural."

Niehaus' home-run call—"It will fly away!"—came from a song he heard while he was in Arizona covering the Mariners' first spring training in 1977.

"An announcer is probably identified by his home-run call more than anything," he said. "I'd been thinking about it for some time, and I was coming back from dinner late one night and the radio was on. They played a song, and the refrain was 'It will fly away.'"

J. Michael Kenyon, who covered the Mariners for the *Seattle Post-Intelligencer*, was riding back to the hotel with Niehaus when they heard the song.

"I said, 'Mike, that's exactly what a home run does when a guy really gets hold of it,'" Niehaus remembers. "I didn't know if I had the guts to use it or not. The next day we were playing San Diego and there were three or four home runs hit, and I decided to use it. It has taken off since then."

The cry Mariners fans love most is Niehaus' grand-slam call. He had long screamed, "It's a grand salami!" for grand slams, but in the mid-1990s he added a popular twist: "Get out the rye bread and mustard, grandma. It's grand salami time!"

"I was thinking one day, 'What goes good with salami?' I came up with that," Niehaus said.

When he first used it during a road telecast, his partner in the booth, Ron Fairly, was shocked.

"Ron thought I had taken a step to the other side of the line," Niehaus said. "He didn't know what the hell I was talking about. But when we got home, that's when we realized that the town had gone crazy with that phrase. The people from the O'Boy! Oberto sausage company sent me these huge salamis."

A Great Honor

As the years passed and Niehaus' popularity grew, Mariners fans hungered for a winning team not only for themselves, but also for the man in the broadcast booth who had suffered through more lousy seasons than anyone.

In 1995, they got their wish when the Mariners made their fabulous comeback to win the AL West. After Randy Johnson struck out Tim Salmon for the final out that clinched the franchise's first division crown, the crowd in the Kingdome celebrated deliriously as the Mariners mobbed each other on the field.

Then something special happened. The crowd turned and faced the broadcast booth, saluting Niehaus with more deafening cheers on a day he'd waited 19 years to experience.

Nothing in baseball, however, became more special to Niehaus than the Mariners' first game at Safeco Field, the new retractable-roof stadium that brought a new era of baseball to Seattle on July 15, 1999. He had taken part in elaborate pregame ceremonies and started back toward the broadcast booth.

Team president Chuck Armstrong stopped him.

"Wait a minute," Armstrong told Niehaus. "We need you to do one more thing."

Armstrong grabbed Niehaus' hand and placed a baseball in it, then told him to walk to the pitcher's mound.

There had been considerable speculation over who would throw out the ceremonial first pitch: One of the original Mariners? A former star player? A government official who helped push the stadium funding and keep baseball in Seattle?

The person who got the ball was the most deserving of them all—Dave Niehaus.

"I hardly made it out to the mound I was sobbing so much," he said.

Tears were flowing, too, on the edge of the field where a cluster of dignitaries had gathered. That's what it meant for them to see Safeco Field become reality and for Niehaus to christen it.

Niehaus composed himself on mound and looked toward the plate, where Tom Foley, the former Speaker of the U.S. House of Representatives, set up to catch his throw. Niehaus flung it high and Foley missed the ball, which rolled to the backstop.

"That ball should have been caught," Niehaus said with a laugh. "It was high, but it wasn't that high."

Clutching the ball tightly after the first-pitch ceremony, Niehaus posed for pictures before hurrying to get off the field and back to the broadcast booth.

"That ball was going to be one of my greatest trophies," he said.

It was until Armstrong grabbed him by the arm again.

"Give the ball to the Speaker, Dave," Armstrong told Niehaus.

He gave the ball to Foley and returned to the broadcast booth without the trophy.

What nobody could take from Niehaus was the memory of that moment, and he will always cherish it.

CHAPTER SEVEN

Young Stars Emerge; Victories Don't

BY THE MID-1980S, the face of the Mariners was changing.

Oh, they still struggled to win games. Between 1983 and 1986 they never won more than 74 games in a season and couldn't finish higher than fifth in the American League West.

Things were different on those teams, though. The Mariners were no longer a collection of has-beens or players who weren't ready for the major leagues. The farm system had begun turning prospects into big leaguers and the young Mariners established an identity among fans with their talent and the hope they provided for the future.

First baseman Alvin Davis hit 27 home runs, drove in 116 runs and won the 1984 American League Rookie of the Year award. Pitcher Mark Langston went 17-10 with a 3.40 ERA—magnificent numbers in the hitter-friendly Kingdome—and he won *The Sporting News* Rookie Pitcher of the Year award. Langston also finished second to Davis in the Rookie of the Year voting.

The mid-'80s Mariners featured players in the beginnings of nice careers: Dave Henderson, Harold Reynolds, Dave Valle, Spike Owen, Jim Presley, Phil Bradley, Ivan Calderon, Danny Tartabull, Mike Moore, Mike Morgan, Matt Young, Edwin Nunez and Jim Beattie. They weren't quite household names in a city that still hadn't fully latched onto Major League Baseball, but they caught the attention of those who did follow the Mariners win or lose.

Dave Valle. *Photo by The Herald of Everett, WA*

"I've been in the game a long time, and it's rare to find a young group like we had then," said Chuck Cottier, who managed the Mariners from 1984-86. "Most of them were brought up through the organization together, so they knew one another. Individually they were outstanding, but as a group they were great. They all liked each other and respected each other and got along well together. That's hard to find with a young group at the major-league level. They were a very, very special group."

They were good, too. Davis, Bradley, Presley, Langston, Reynolds, Calderon, Tartabull, Moore and Morgan went on to become All-Stars. Unfortunately for Mariners fans, many of those players had their best years with other teams because management wouldn't sign them to long-term contracts to stay in Seattle.

Had the organization kept the young talent together, Cottier is convinced the Mariners would have produced their first winning record long before that finally happened in 1991. Owner George Argyros didn't believe in signing players to long-term contracts, and when free agency loomed for the talented young Mariners, the club often traded them away or let them sign elsewhere.

"In my heart, I truly believe we could have been as good as Oakland was in their heyday," Cottier said. "Those kids would have been outstanding here. You saw what happened to them when they went to other organizations. They had nice careers and wound up as millionaires with other teams. But it cheated the fans in Seattle because when the players left, the fans lost that identity."

• Center fielder Dave Henderson was the Mariners' first-round draft pick in 1977, and he became a fixture in the outfield from 1982-86 before they traded him and shortstop Spike Owen to the Red Sox for shortstop Rey Quinones and cash. Henderson became an All-Star in 1991 with the Oakland A's and played in four World Series with the Red Sox and A's.

• Second baseman Danny Tartabull played in Seattle from 1984-86, but the Mariners traded him to the Royals before his free-agent season in exchange for Scott Bankhead, Steve Shields, and Mike Kingery. Tartabull batted .270 for the Mariners in 1986, his first full major-league season at age 23, and hit 25 home runs with 91 runs batted in. He played 10 more seasons, hitting 30 or more homers three times and driving in 100 or more runs five times. He made the AL All-Star team in 1991.

• Left fielder Phil Bradley was a star quarterback at the University of Missouri who played four full seasons with the Mariners. He beat the Mariners twice in arbitration, then was traded to the Phillies before the 1988 season for Glenn Wilson, Mike Jackson, and minor leaguer Dave

Phil Bradley. *Photo by The Herald of Everett, WA*

Brundage. Bradley batted .300 in 1985 and .310 in 1986, setting career highs of 26 homers and 88 RBIs in '85, when he made the All-Star team.

• Right fielder Ivan Calderon broke in with the Mariners in 1984 and batted .286 in 67 games in '85. The Mariners sent him to the White Sox midway through the 1986 season as the player to be named later in a trade that brought catcher Scott Bradley to Seattle. Calderon became an All-Star with the Expos in 1991, when he batted .300 for the only time in his career.

•Third baseman Jim Presley played six seasons with the Mariners, from 1984-89, before they traded him to the Atlanta Braves after the 1990 season.

• Pitcher Mike Moore, the first overall pick in the 1981 draft, won 17 games and pitched 14 complete games for the Mariners in 1985. He signed with the A's as a free agent before the 1989 season and won 19 games that year, pitching a workhorse 241⅔ innings.

• Second baseman Harold Reynolds, the second overall pick in the 1980 draft, was one of the few young stars who played the biggest part of his career in Seattle. He was a Mariner from 1983-92, then played for the Orioles in 1993 and the Angels in 1994 before retiring.

Reynolds, a native of Corvallis, Oregon, became a crowd favorite with his speed and defense. He led the league with 60 steals in 1987 and 11 triples in 1988, he won Gold Gloves at second base in 1988, '89, and '90, and he represented the Mariners at the All-Star Game in 1987 and '88.

"Harold came along and hit .370 one year in Triple-A," Cottier said. "We brought him up and he developed into a very consistent player."

Mr. Mariner: The First-Class Alvin Davis

Alvin Davis, selected by the Mariners in the sixth round of the 1982 draft, could do so many things well. He hit for average and power, he flashed a nice glove around first base and, perhaps his best-known trait, he was one of the nicest players ever to wear the Mariners uniform.

If only he could run.

Speed wasn't Davis' game and it cost him. He rarely beat out infield grounders to the holes, and pitchers didn't hesitate to walk him because they knew he was no threat to steal. He was

Alvin Davis. *Photo by The Herald of Everett, WA*

consistently among the American League leaders in walks and on-base percentage.

Davis played eight seasons with the Mariners, won the American League Rookie of the Year award in 1984 and, after one year with the California Angels, finished his major-league career with 160 home runs, 683 runs batted in and a .280 batting average.

"I believe he could have added 20 to 30 more hits a year if he'd had any speed," outfielder John Moses said.

Davis became the Mariners' first big offensive star. He homered off Dennis Eckersley in his first major-league game and went on to bat .284 with 27 home runs and 116 RBIs as a rookie in 1984.

"He was a leader," Moses said. "He was a quiet leader; his bat spoke for itself."

Chuck Cottier said it was a privilege to be Davis' skipper during the three seasons he managed the Mariners.

"He came up and had that great rookie year, and he continued to play well," Cottier said. "He was a superstar in all aspects of his game except one. He was a slow runner. But he was a good fielder, a great hitter, and he hit for power."

In addition to what Davis gave the Mariners on the field, he was a classy representative off it. Broadcaster Dave Niehaus nicknamed Davis "Mr. Mariner" because he represented the franchise with such a positive attitude. In 1997, the Mariners made him the first inductee into the team's Hall of Fame.

"He was an All-American kid," Niehaus said. "It seemed natural to call him Mr. Mariner."

What Alvin Davis' teammates remember best about him was the joy he brought to the ballpark.

"Alvin and I spent half a season together in Double-A ball before I got called up to the big leagues," Moses said. "We were on a 13-hour bus ride from Massachusetts to Buffalo, New York, and I mean, that was a long, hard ride. But every time I looked back at him on that bus, Alvin had a smile on his face. He was smiling for 13 hours.

"He loved the game so much."

Mark Langston: Iron Man on the Mound

Even in the mid-1980s, when pitchers who started a game actually saw the end of it, Mark Langston's numbers were impressive.

The left-hander was the Mariners' iron man in 1987, his fourth major-league season, when he pitched 14 complete games and

Mark Langston. *Photo by The Herald of Everett, WA*

worked 272 innings to set a franchise record that may never be broken.

Langston won 17 games in his first season, 1984, and captured *The Sporting News* American League Rookie Pitcher of the Year award. He kept getting better, building up not only victories, but an amazing record of durability.

Langston pitched 200 or more innings in 10 of his 16 major-league seasons, and in his five and a half seasons with the Mariners he pitched 225 innings in 1984, 239⅓ in 1986, 272 in 1987 and 261⅓ in 1988.

"He was a workhorse," Moses said. "That's the difference between nowadays and back then. Here's a guy who would give you seven, eight solid innings. Now, guys just want to get through the fifth so they can get the decision one way or the other. Langston never thought about that."

Langston's only down year was 1985, when he labored through his second major-league season with a 7-14 record. It didn't surprise his manager, Chuck Cottier, and the Mariners decided to give Langston a breather by skipping a start late in the season.

"For a young player, getting through a 162-game schedule at the major-league level can be difficult," Cottier said. "It was the latter part of August and we were going to skip his turn in the rotation to let his arm rest a little."

George Argyros, the team owner, had a different idea: Send Langston to Class-AAA Calgary and have him pitch there. After all, if the club was paying the guy, why not keep working him?

"But George," Cottier told the owner. "This is the kind of kid you develop your organization around. We need to be careful with him. He doesn't need to be in Triple-A, and if you send him there, you can send me there with him."

Cottier won that dispute, and Langston never spent another day in the minors.

Langston had racked up 73⅓ innings and an impressive 3.56 ERA through 10 starts in 1989, but the Mariners, knowing they weren't going to compete in what would be a big-money free-agent market, traded him away. On May 25 they shipped Langston and a player to be named later (pitcher Mike Campbell) to the Montreal Expos for three young, barely known pitchers whose uncertain future made Mariners fans uneasy.

The Mariners received a couple of 24-year-old right-handers, Brian Holman and Gene Harris, and a lanky, hard-throwing—but wild—left-hander named Randy Johnson.

Over time, the trade became a true fleecing of the Expos.

Langston played the rest of that season with Montreal before signing as a free agent with the California Angels, where he continued his iron-man efforts by pitching 200 or more innings in five of the next seven seasons. Johnson, meanwhile, corralled his control and became the cornerstone of the Mariners' division championship teams in 1995 and 1997.

CHAPTER EIGHT

Bizarre Moments On and Off the Field

THIRTY YEARS OF BASEBALL in Seattle have brought the usual assortment of interesting behavior by players and incidents off the field, some worth laughing about now and others that still make people cringe.

Bob Kearney was a light-hitting catcher who played eight seasons in the majors, the last four with the Mariners from 1984-87. He was an adequate backstop who was nicknamed "Sarge" and is remembered as much for what he said as the things he did.

"He was really smart IQ-wise, very intelligent. But he also was very, very funny," said longtime trainer Rick Griffin, who compiled a list of "Kearney-isms" during the catcher's time with the Mariners. "He would say things that would make you shake your head."

Former manager Chuck Cottier remembers the day Kearney replaced his eyeglasses with a pair of contact lenses.

"He'd been trying different types of lenses—hard, soft, whatever—trying to find a pair that worked for him," Cottier said. "We were playing a Sunday afternoon game in Milwaukee and Bob comes up to me and says, 'Chuck, I've got my contacts now and they're the best I've ever had.'"

Kearney, who'd caught the night before, didn't start that afternoon's game, but Cottier had him warm up the pitchers in the bullpen to get accustomed to the new lenses in daylight. Late in the game, Cottier plugged Kearney into the lineup for defensive reasons.

Kearney was behind the plate when Mariners reliever Ed Vande Berg gave up a high popup with runners on second and third base and two outs.

"Sarge circled around it but he didn't come near it," Cottier said. "Vande Berg had to catch it off his shoetops for the third out."

Kearney trotted back to the dugout, looked at Cottier and delivered one of his famed Kearney-isms.

"Skip," he said. "That sun looks a lot brighter in the daytime than it is at night."

Mariners president Chuck Armstrong was at spring training one March in Tempe, Arizona, when he decided to strike up a conversation with Kearney.

"Where are you staying down here?" Armstrong asked.

"I'm living in this condo, right on the ground floor," Kearney said. "It's great because it's so warm here at night and I can walk right outside to work on my tan."

Armstrong was stumped. "You're working on your tan? At night?"

"Yeah, the moonrays are perfect for that," Kearney said.

"Moonrays?" Armstrong asked.

"Yeah, there's a full moon now," Kearney explained. "The rays from the sun are bouncing off the moon, and I get a tan."

Talented, Unpredictable Rey Quinones

The Mariners thought they were upgrading themselves at shortstop in 1986 when general manager Dick Balderson obtained highly regarded shortstop Rey Quinones from the Red Sox. In exchange, the Mariners traded away solid little shortstop Spike Owen and talented young outfielder Dave Henderson.

The trade left the Mariners with one of the more disappointing players in franchise history. Quinones had remarkable talent but his inconsistent behavior on and off the field wound up hurting the Mariners and himself.

"To this day, I think he is one of the most talented guys I've ever seen," trainer Rick Griffin said. "But he didn't really care about playing the game. He enjoyed being there, but he didn't want to play."

Rey Quinones. *Photo by The Herald of Everett, WA*

Quinones played only four seasons in the major leagues, including 311 games with the Mariners from 1986-89 before they traded him to the Pittsburgh Pirates. The Pirates released him midway through the 1989 season and he never played in the majors again.

How talented was Quinones?

Griffin remembers two games, one in Detroit and one in New York, when Quinones announced in the dugout, "This game is over, I'm going to hit a home run." Then he went to the plate and did it.

Defensively, Quinones was one of the game's best talents.

"He could stand at home plate in the Kingdome and throw the ball into the second deck in center field," Griffin said. "He had the best arm of an infielder that I've ever seen. It's a sad deal. You always wondered what kind of a player he could have been, but he just didn't have his priorities in order."

Despite all that talent, Quinones never showed a burning desire to play. He showed up late for spring training in 1987, telling the Mariners he had visa problems.

"Uh, Rey," team president Chuck Armstrong told him, "you're from Puerto Rico. You don't need a visa."

The writers who covered the Mariners that year won't forget the day Quinones arrived.

"We got a call one night that Rey was back in the fold, and that we could come up to talk with him," said Larry LaRue of *The News Tribune* of Tacoma.

LaRue, Jim Street of the *Seattle Post-Intelligencer* and Bob Finnigan of the *Seattle Times* went up to public relations director Dave Aust's hotel suite. They experienced one of the strangest interviews of their careers.

"Rey was lying on his back, flat on the floor the whole time," LaRue said. "We conducted the interview that way, the three of us and Aust standing above him."

Among other things, Quinones told the writers that he didn't need baseball, saying he owned a liquor store in Puerto Rico and could live off that.

Later that season, Armstrong was walking through the Mariners' clubhouse before a game when manager Dick Williams called him into his office. Armstrong walked in and saw Quinones there with Williams and general manager Dick Balderson.

"Rey, tell Chuck what you just told us," Williams said.

"I'm a good shortstop, right?" Quinones said.

"You're a very good shortstop, Rey," Armstrong told him.

"I could be the best shortstop in the American League," Quinones said.

"Yes you could," Armstrong replied.

"I'm so good," Quinones continued, "that I don't need to play every day."

Armstrong was stunned as Quinones continued.

"I don't need to play every day, and you have other guys who should play so they can get better," Quinones said. "So I don't need to play tonight."

Williams reworked the lineup, replacing Quinones at shortstop with Domingo Ramos.

"Rey wasn't even in the dugout during the early part of the game, Ramos was having a great game," Armstrong said. "He made a couple of great plays in the field, and he tripled and doubled."

Seeing that, Quinones put on his uniform and appeared in the dugout, telling Williams that he was ready to play.

"No you're not," Williams told him. "You're out of uniform. No hat."

Quinones returned to the clubhouse for a hat, then reported to Williams again. Williams told him to take a seat, that Ramos would play the rest of the game.

Other players on the team began calling Quinones "Wally Pipp," and he had only one question.

"Who's Wally Pipp?" he asked.

Most Disappointing Manager

The Mariners wallowed near last place in the 1980 season when the club fired Darrell Johnson, their manager since the franchise began in 1977, and replaced him with a man they hoped would take the club in a new direction.

Former Dodgers speedster Maury Wills became the second Mariners manager, and the front office saw him as a person who would instill the up-tempo style that made him such a great player. Besides that, Wills could engage the fans with his entertaining stories.

Unknown to the Mariners at the time, alcohol and drugs were taking a firm grip on Wills. Whether it was the addiction or his inexperience as a manager, Wills was unprepared and overmatched as a manager, and his time was marked by several unusual incidents.

"He probably was the most disappointing manager in our history," broadcaster Dave Niehaus said. "He came with the reputation of being a baseball guy, but little did we know what he was going through. Some of the things he did were just unbelievable."

During one spring training game in 1981, Wills went to the mound to make a pitching change and signaled for a right-hander. There wasn't a right-hander warming up.

Later that spring, Wills sent catcher Brad Gulden to pinch hit against a left-handed pitcher, even though Gulden was a left-handed hitter. After the at-bat, Wills was irate.

"Why didn't you tell me you were left-handed?" he asked Gulden.

Niehaus remembered asking Wills about his outfielders going into the 1981 spring camp, and the answer surprised him.

"We've got that guy in left field who's going to be a pretty good ballplayer," Wills said. "He had a pretty good year last year and he's going to be the backbone of our outfield."

Niehaus, puzzled, asked, "You mean Leon Roberts?"

"Yeah, Leon Roberts," Wills said.

Roberts wasn't even with the Mariners, having been traded two months earlier to the Texas Rangers in an 11-player deal.

The most often-told story involving Wills and the Mariners occurred on April 25, 1981, during a series at the Kingdome against the Oakland A's. Oakland manager Billy Martin had complained during the series opener that the Mariners' Tom Paciorek was striding out of the batter's box when he hit the ball and should have been called out.

The Mariners faced A's breaking ball specialist Rick Langford the next night, and Wills thought he had the perfect solution for Paciorek. He ordered Wilber Loo, the head groundskeeper at the Kingdome, to extend the batter's box several inches toward the mound. That way, Paciorek would have plenty of room to cheat up and hack at Langford's pitches before they broke.

"I remember looking at the box thinking, 'There's something wrong with that,'" said Randy Adamack, the Mariners' public relations director. "Then I looked down and Billy Martin was pointing to it and talking with the umpires about it."

Umpire Bill Kunkel measured the batter's box and, sure enough, it was a foot longer than the regulation six feet.

Wills was fined $500 by the American League and suspended for two games. Less than two weeks later, the last-place Mariners fired Wills and replaced him with Rene Lachemann.

Not everyone was happy to see Wills leave. Julio Cruz, a young infielder with great speed, became one of the league's best base-stealers under him.

"He was really good for me," Cruz said. "I had never stolen a base off a lefty, but Maury would bring me out early and teach me how to do it. I wish he had stayed longer. What he did, he did to himself, and I didn't pay that much attention to those things. But I know he had a lot to give to the game."

He Wasn't a Football Hero

The Mariners sought some left-handed punch for their lineup in 2000, and they obtained outfielder Al Martin from the Padres in a trade-deadline deal. What the Mariners got was a ballplayer who had plenty of controversy swirling off the field.

The Mariners already knew about a bigamy incident involving Martin, who was arrested early in 2000 on charges that he and a woman claiming to be his wife had gotten into a fight. The woman, Shawn Haggerty-Martin, claimed they were married in 1998 in Las Vegas. Martin didn't deny that he attended a wedding with her, but he didn't realize the ceremony was real. All the while, he was married to another woman.

The two-wives-at-once episode wasn't all that raised eyebrows.

Martin had long contended that he played football at the University of Southern California. Media guides with the Pirates, Padres, and Mariners included information—provided by Martin—saying he played at USC. During interviews, he would tell stories of making tackles in big games for the Trojans.

The subject came up after Martin collided with Mariners shortstop Carlos Guillen during the 2000 season. Describing the collision to a *Seattle Times* reporter, Martin likened it to a USC football game in 1986 when he tried to tackle Leroy Hoard of Michigan.

The *Times* did some checking and learned that USC didn't play Michigan that year. In fact, Martin never played a down at USC and there was no record of him being on the team.

Confronted with that, Martin told the *Times* he would supply proof that he played for USC. He never did.

CHAPTER NINE

How the Mariners Almost Passed on Ken Griffey Jr.

THE MARINERS HAD THE FIRST PICK IN THE 1987 DRAFT, and it seemed obvious to everyone in baseball who they would take.

A skinny high school kid in Cincinnati had amazed every scout who'd watched him show off his powerful swing, his cat-like ability to play center field, and his unbridled joy for the game.

There wasn't much doubt that Ken Griffey Jr., the son of Reds great Ken Griffey, would be a star.

"The first time I saw him was at a tournament in Texas when he was only about 15 years old, and he was the best player," said Roger Jongewaard, the Mariners' scouting director in 1985. "He was the youngest player on the field, but he was the best player. He was special."

Two years later, when another last-place finish netted the Mariners the first pick in the 1987 draft, taking Griffey seemed like the no-brainer of all no-brainers. Team owner George Argyros, however, wasn't so certain that Griffey was a wise choice.

Argyros felt the Mariners had been burned the previous year when they used their first-round pick on highly regarded high school shortstop Patrick Lennon, who had off-field issues and never developed into the star they thought he would become.

"I wanted Junior desperately, and all our scouts backed me up," Jongewaard said. "But George wanted a college guy."

Argyros, a Southern California real-estate developer, favored a right-handed pitcher out of Cal State-Fullerton named Mike Harkey.

"I just can't do that, George," Jongewaard told Argyros. "This Griffey is a special guy."

Compounding Argyros' uncertainty over Griffey was that he wasn't eligible during his high school season because of his grades at Moeller High School in Cincinnati.

"We wanted him, but it's hard to take a guy No. 1 who isn't playing high school baseball," Jongewaard said. "I asked the athletic director what was wrong with Kenny, why he couldn't stay eligible. His theory was that Moeller is a football school and there was pressure for Kenny to play football, and maybe this was his way of not having to play football."

That made sense, but the Mariners also became concerned over Griffey's low scores on the mental aptitude tests that they gave him. Dick Balderson, the Mariners' general manager at the time, believed those tests told a lot about a potential player's ability to play a mentally difficult game.

Jongewaard had spoken to enough of Griffey's high school coaches to know that he was a smart kid, so the low test scores didn't make sense.

"School just wasn't a top priority with him," said Mike Cameron, the longtime baseball coach at Moeller High School. "I kept telling Kenny that the spring was real important as far as where he would go in the draft, and there was also college if he wanted to go there.

"Then he just looked at me and said, 'Coach, I was born to play baseball.'"

The Mariners soon learned that Griffey, while vitally interested in baseball, had no patience for sitting through their long test.

"He wasn't even completing it," Jongewaard said. "He'd see that it had 90 questions and give up on it."

Jongewaard, believing Griffey could score much higher on the test if he gave it a serious effort, asked him to take it again.

"I've already done it for the (scouting) bureau and I've done it for you guys," Griffey said. "No more."

"But do you really want to be No. 1?" Jongewaard asked.

Griffey said he did.

"Then we have to do this again," Jongewaard said.

Jongewaard told Mariners scout Tom Mooney to give Griffey the test again and let him have all the time he needed to answer the questions. Most importantly, Mooney wouldn't allow Griffey to speed through the test just to get it over with.

They had gotten about halfway through the multiple-choice test when Griffey wanted to take a break and get something to drink. They both left the room, and when Mooney returned, Griffey had sped through most of the remaining questions and marked the answers.

"He just guessed at them, putting Xs in all the columns straight down the page," Jongewaard said. "He didn't have the patience to finish it."

Mooney wouldn't let Griffey get away with it this time, and he read the questions and made him finish the test. Jongewaard doesn't remember how Griffey scored, "but he did OK. That was a hurdle we cleared."

It wasn't the final one, however. Jongewaard still needed to convince his skeptical owner, George Argyros, that Griffey was worth the No. 1 pick in the draft.

"George, we can't afford not to take this guy," Jongewaard told him. "He is that special."

"OK, but it will be your ass if he doesn't do well," Argyros told Jongewaard. "He'd better do well. He'd better do special well, if you say he's so special."

Jongewaard had heard the "this will be your ass" speech from Argyros before, and he wasn't deterred. Then Argyros gave one more ultimatum: "You can take him, but you've got to have him signed. He's got to agree to our deal prior to the draft."

Jongewaard wasn't sure he could overcome this hurdle.

Jongewaard sent one of the Mariners' top scouts, Bob Harrison, to Cincinnati to meet with the Griffey family and get Junior's name on a contract. Jongewaard was on the phone constantly with Harrison.

"When we opened the negotiations, Junior wanted a new Porsche and all these things," Jongewaard said. "We couldn't do any of the things he asked for."

The Mariners showed the Griffeys what the Pirates gave Jeff King, the No. 1 pick in 1986, and pointed out that their offer was an increase over that money. What Griffey had to decide, the Mariners told him, was how badly he wanted to be the first player selected in the draft.

Ken Griffey Sr. turned to his son and asked, "Junior, do you want to be No. 1?"

Junior's response: "Oh yeah."

"I thought we had a chance then," Jongewaard said.

On the day before the draft, the Griffeys agreed verbally to the Mariners' $160,000 offer, but they told Harrison that they wanted to wait until the next morning to sign.

"But Bob," Jongewaard said. "By then they will change their minds 10 times and everyone they've talked with will tell them to get more money."

"No, Roger," Harrison said. "They gave me their word."

"This is the key guy," Jongewaard told Harrison. "If you get this done, I'll have a limo at the airport when you get back to Seattle tomorrow."

Harrison got only a couple hours of sleep before he met the Griffeys the next morning, when they indeed kept their word and Junior signed the contract. Harrison rushed to the airport for his flight back to Seattle, eagerly awaiting the limo ride from Sea-Tac Airport and a hero's welcome when he reached the Mariners' downtown offices.

When Harrison arrived, no limo, no cab, nothing was waiting for him. He called Jongewaard.

"Roger, I just landed and nobody was waiting for me," Harrison said. "I thought you were going to have a limo."

Jongewaard, thrilled and relieved to have Griffey signed, had continued preparing for the draft and became so occupied with that task that he forgot about his promise to Harrison.

"I'm sorry," he told Harrison. "Here I am one minute promising you the moon, and the next you're yesterday's news."

The Making of a Superstar

Mike Cameron, the coach at Moeller, had heard about Ken Griffey Jr.'s great swing long before the kid joined the high school team.

"There were stories of him as a 12-year-old hitting balls farther than most 21-year-olds," Cameron said.

He couldn't wait for Griffey's first high school practice to see the special things this player could accomplish. Instead, Cameron was shocked at what Griffey couldn't do.

"It was before the season started and we had stations the guys would rotate to," Cameron said. "At one of them were batting tees. He got up there and he put a ball on the tee and he would swing and miss it. He kept missing and I thought, 'Oh my gosh! I'd heard all these stories about him, and he can't even hit the ball off a tee?'"

Cameron decided to approach Griffey with a few tee-ball tips.

"Hey Kenny, you've got to work on this, so let's try some things to help you hit the ball off the tee," Cameron told him.

Griffey balked.

"Coach," he said. "The Griffeys, we don't swing off a tee."

Cameron and his assistant coach, Paul Smith, weren't sure what to do.

"Then I remembered a very successful college coach once told me that until a player experiences failure, you won't be able to change him," Cameron said. "Kenny never had failure in high school. In batting practice, he could put the ball exactly where he wanted."

Four years later, at the Kingdome in Seattle, Griffey took batting practice with the Mariners not long after the draft. First-round picks would typically work out with the big-league club for a day before joining their minor-league teams, and often those players were a mass of nerves. Not Griffey.

"He had been around big-league teams all his life with his dad, so he wasn't intimidated," scouting director Roger Jongewaard said. "He jumped into the cage and hit more balls out than Alvin Davis or anybody we had. He looked like a better batting-practice hitter with better power than anybody, and he was only 17."

Mariners outfielder John Moses remembers being awe-struck by Griffey's batting-practice session.

"He was in my hitting group, and right away he hit a ball into the third deck," Moses said. "With a wood bat. Right out of high school. All I could think was that I probably wouldn't be here the next year."

Moses was right; the Mariners released him after the 1987 season. Two seasons later, Griffey was the starting center fielder.

Griffey's Climb to the Majors

After the draft, the Mariners assigned Ken Griffey Jr. to their short-season Class-A team in Bellingham, Washington, for his first pro season in 1987.

The transition was difficult. He was a 17-year-old playing with and against college-age players who were five and six years older. Griffey's numbers were strong—he batted .313 for the season—but it wasn't a fun summer.

"After about two weeks, he was ready to come home and he was going to chuck baseball because he was homesick," said Mike Cameron, his high school coach. "Kids at that age think they're ready to live on their own. But it's a shock because Mom's not there to make the meals."

Roger Jongewaard, the Mariners' scouting director, had another theory: Griffey simply was too good for his competition and wasn't challenged.

"He was too good for the league and he got bored with it," Jongewaard said. "Late in the season, he was trying to see how far he could hit the ball and he was getting himself out."

Jongewaard made a trip to Bellingham to talk with Griffey about it.

"Junior, I'm disappointed you're not a better player than this," Jongewaard told him. "I'd heard so many good things about you."

"It's not that much fun here," Griffey told him.

"All it was," Jongewaard said, "is that he was bored at that level. And that was a college-level league."

Griffey played at High-A San Bernardino in 1988, hitting .338 in 58 games, then was promoted to Double-A Vermont. He only made it through 17 games there before a back injury ended his season.

Still, the Mariners were enthused that Griffey had performed so well at every level he played, and they invited him to spring training the next year. The plan was to give Griffey a taste of the big-league camp, then have him spend the rest of the year with the Triple-A team in Calgary.

"This will be a good thing," Jongewaard told general manager Woody Woodward. "We'll get Junior to Calgary and he'll hit a lot of home runs in that little ballpark, and it'll help our relationship with the Calgary franchise."

Woodward couldn't disagree, but he couldn't agree, either. Griffey was having an exceptional spring camp, and Woodward couldn't see sending him to the minors.

"You're right, I'd like to get another year for him in the minors," Woodward said. "But he is our best player in the major-league camp. How do you send out your best player?"

Griffey never spent another day in the minor leagues.

Manager Jim Lefebvre put him in the Opening Day lineup and, at age 19, Griffey went 1-for-3 at Oakland in his first major-league game. He didn't get another hit the rest of that series and only one the rest of the Mariners' opening road trip, going 2-for-19.

The Mariners limped into their home opener with a 1-5 record, but Griffey provided a perfect lift in his first game at the Kingdome on April 10, 1989.

On the first pitch of his first home at-bat, Griffey launched a drive off White Sox pitcher Eric King for his first major-league home run, helping the Mariners beat Chicago 6-5. The next night, he homered again off Chicago right-hander Shawn Hillegas in the Mariners' 8-6 loss.

As Griffey's season progressed, he was everything the Mariners wanted. He batted .325 the first month of the season and was holding up well through the grind of everyday play and cross-country travel. Then he broke the little finger on his left hand on July 24 in Chicago and was placed on the disabled list. Several media reports said he injured himself punching a wall in his hotel room.

Griffey batted just .214 in the 39 games he played after returning from the injury, but he finished the season with respectable numbers nonetheless, especially for a teenage rookie—16 home runs, 61 runs batted in, 23 doubles, 18 steals, and a .264 batting average.

"When he stepped onto the field, that was his escape and you could tell in the way he played how much he enjoyed it," right fielder Jay Buhner said. "He'd show up every day and do something that made you say, 'Wow!'"

Griffey's potent swing and his ability to play center field grabbed the attention of fans like never before in the history of the franchise. Families would interrupt dinner during Griffey's at-bats so they could watch him on TV. Nobody wanted to miss a long home run or a highlight-reel defensive play. And his teenage energy and joy for the game captivated young fans, and No. 24 "Griffey" jerseys became part of their attire.

"You could sense the level of interest rising," said Randy Adamack, the Mariners' director of communications. "He had marquee value, he was from our farm system, and he was good. He became a national story that brought the spotlight to the franchise for really the first time."

On the field, even Griffey's teammates were amazed at what they were witnessing on an almost daily basis.

"I had the best seat in the house to watch him," catcher Dave Valle said. "I saw the ball leave the bat, and it would look like it was going to be a double, and all of a sudden he would come flying out of nowhere, climbing walls in right-center, making that spider-man catch.

"Or he would be stealing a home run off Jesse Barfield at Yankee Stadium."

There's no better definition of Griffey's flair for the dramatic, his athleticism, and his enthusiasm than the Barfield catch. He did it early in his second season, in 1990, on baseball's biggest stage—Yankee Stadium.

Yankees outfielder Jesse Barfield launched a drive to deep left-center field in the bottom of the fourth inning and Griffey, with his unbridled speed and no fear of the wall, blazed a trail to the deepest part of Yankee Stadium. He timed his leap perfectly, reached high over the wall and caught the ball, robbing Barfield of a home run.

"The TV replays of that don't do it justice," said Yankees third baseman Mike Blowers, who became a Mariners teammate with

Griffey a few years later. "Junior was shifted around to right-center and he had to run a whole football field to get to that ball. All Jesse could do was laugh."

The lasting image of the Barfield catch wasn't what Griffey did while he made that play, but his reaction afterward. He came down with the ball for the third out of the inning and sprinted back to the dugout holding the ball aloft, smiling all the way back.

"Junior didn't just do things like that every once in a while," Valle said. "He was doing something like that every night."

This One's For Dad

Ken Griffey Jr. not only spread his name across the Mariners' record books, he became the standard across baseball for most of his 11 seasons in Seattle.

He led the American League in home runs in 1994, '97, '98 and '99, including 56 homers in both 1997 and 1998. He hit 40 or more home runs in six of his final seven seasons with the Mariners, missing that mark only in 1995 when he missed most of the season because of a broken wrist.

He was a 10-time All-Star as a Mariner, winning the All-Star Game MVP in 1992. He won the American League MVP award in 1997, won 10 straight Gold Gloves from 1990-99 and seven Silver Slugger awards.

"He's one of those few guys, when he wanted to do something, he could do it," Mariners right fielder Jay Buhner said. "When he called a shot, he did it. He would say, 'This guy has this pitch and he's going to do this today, and I'm going to take him deep.' And then he would. When Junior got hot, oh my God. He could carry a team for weeks."

Amid all the home runs, awards, and spectacular plays Griffey made, nothing topped the last day of August in 1991.

That night in the Kingdome against the Kansas City Royals, Griffey started in his usual spot in center field and his father, Ken Griffey Sr., started in left field. It was the first time in major-league history that a father and son played for the same team in the same game. Two days earlier, the Mariners signed Ken Griffey Sr. shortly after he was released by the Cincinnati Reds.

Ken Griffey Sr. (left) and Ken Griffey Jr. joke around before the start of the game. *Photo courtesy of the Seattle Mariners*

Father batted second and son batted third in that historic game against the Kansas City Royals, and in the first inning against pitcher Storm Davis, the Griffeys hit back-to-back singles.

Two weeks later, on September 14 at Anaheim, they made history again.

Ken Griffey Sr. batted against Angels right-hander Kirk McCaskill with a runner on first base, and he smashed a two-run home run over the center-field fence. After he crossed home plate, the father trotted past his son in the on-deck circle and gave the kid some advice.

"That's how you do it, Son," Ken Griffey Sr. said.

Junior then dug in against McCaskill and hit a similar bolt, his 20th home run of the season, to nearly the same spot over the center-field fence. When he arrived back at the Mariners' dugout, Junior told Dad one thing.

"That's how you do it, Dad," he said.

Then they embraced.

Junior and Jay: Best Buddies

Two young ballplayers from vastly different backgrounds—Ken Griffey Jr., the kid from Cincinnati, and Jay Buhner, the lanky Texan—didn't seem like the obvious twosome to form an unbreakable bond.

But that's what developed after Buhner came to the Mariners late in the 1988 season in a trade with the Yankees.

"They didn't have anything in common," trainer Rick Griffin said. "But in spring training they started joking around and they hit it off."

Buhner often said, "Junior is my brother from a different mother."

When Griffey bought a home in a suburb east of Seattle, Buhner bought the house next door.

"We shared a lot of the same interests off the baseball field, and that was a key to our friendship," Buhner said.

They would travel to the Kingdome together, and those 30-minute drives offered a chance to talk about things other than baseball. Griffey badly needed that, Buhner said.

"There was such a tug and pull on Junior whenever he went to the ballpark," Buhner said. "I was able to take his mind away from that part of it. Our relationship got to the point where he could talk about things. He couldn't let his guard down around too many people because he always had to be careful about what he said and what he did.

"Plus," Buhner added, "I gave him a lot of crap."

Buhner was the Mariners' all-time great jokester/intimidator/motivator, and just because Griffey was one of the biggest stars in all of sports didn't make him immune from Buhner's abuse.

"I didn't let him get away with a bunch of crap, and I wasn't afraid to jump his ass," Buhner said. "But it was vice versa, too."

During one game in Yankee Stadium, for example, the bleacher creatures were up to their usual abuse, giving Griffey a hard time.

"F--- you, Junior! F--- you, Junior!" they chanted.

Griffey looked back to the crowd and smiled, then pointed to right field where Buhner stood.

Within seconds, the bleacher crowd shifted to a new target. "F--- you, Buhner! F--- you, Buhner!" they chanted.

Buhner and Griffey also pushed each other to become better ballplayers.

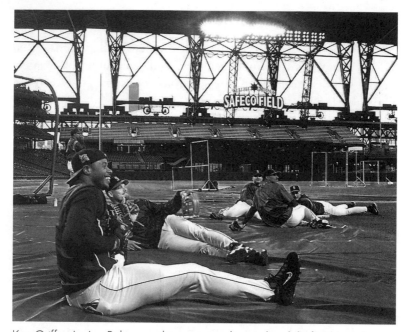

Ken Griffey Jr., Jay Buhner and teammates share a laugh before a workout at Safeco Field. The Mariners tested the new ballpark before it opened to the public in July 1999. *Photo by Dan Bates/The Herald of Everett, WA*

They would play their own personal game within the game, tallying points for such accomplishments as base hits, doubles, triples, home runs, and RBIs. At the end of the night, the one with the most points bought the other dinner.

To Stretch, Or Not to Stretch

Ken Griffey Jr. bragged that he never lifted a weight, and he said he didn't believe in stretching.

"Does a cheetah stretch before it chases its prey?" he once asked.

When Griffey suffered strains, pulls and tears after the Mariners traded him to the Reds, critics pointed to his disdain for weightlifting and stretching as the reasons his body was breaking down.

The trainers who worked with Griffey during his years with the Mariners strongly dispute that theory.

"People say he didn't work hard, but he did. He worked very hard," said Rick Griffin, the Mariners' head trainer. "The work he did was functional and related to baseball. He didn't go into the weight room and do a lot of stuff, but he did things that were related to him being a better player."

As for stretching, when Griffey said he didn't believe in it, that mostly was a bluff to the media, Griffin said.

"He is the most flexible player I've ever had," Griffin said. "He stretched all the time."

Griffey often would have Griffey stand in the dugout with his back to the wall, then he'd take a leg and pull it above his head and touch his toe on the dugout wall.

"That's how flexible his legs were," Griffin said. "He always stretched, he always did things for his wrists, knees, and legs. People just didn't see it."

So Long, Seattle

Ken Griffey Jr. clearly wasn't a happy player by 1999, when the Mariners played half the season in the Kingdome and half at Safeco Field, their new retractable-roof ballpark.

He rarely took pregame batting practice, especially in the second half of the year, because of sore legs. That, and questions about where he would play after his contract expired, wore on him. He also wasn't enamored with the new stadium.

"Four-hundred million dollars and no heat!" he said often.

He could have said, "Four-hundred million and no power alley!"

Safeco Field, built across the street from the Kingdome, couldn't have been more different than the Mariners' original climate-controlled, hitter-friendly ballpark. It featured natural grass and outfield dimensions so vast that balls with home-run distance in the Kingdome would die on the warning track at Safeco Field. The marine air and a breeze off nearby Puget Sound further contributed to the new ballpark's reputation as a palace for pitchers, not hitters.

"Junior saw the park being built, and he thought it was too big," said Roger Jongewaard, the Mariners' scouting director.

There was a growing sense that Griffey wanted to play for a team closer to his off-season home near Orlando, and that his preference was a team that held its spring training camp in Florida.

As a 10-and-5 player (10 years in the major leagues, five with the same team) he had veto power over any trade. Essentially, Griffey could name his next team, and he did, giving the Mariners a list of four teams he would accept as trade partners—the Reds, Mets, Braves, and Astros.

Deals with the Mets, Braves, and Astros were discussed, with no progress. Griffey finally put his foot down and said the Reds, who he'd grown up around with his father, were the only team he'd approve.

On February 9, 2000, the Mariners and Reds worked out a tentative agreement to trade Griffey to his hometown team. The Reds had 72 hours to put together a contract extension with Griffey, who said he would accept less than market value to play in Cincinnati. During the 1999 season, he had turned down an eight-year, $148-million contract extension from the Mariners.

Griffey and the Reds agreed to a nine-year contract for $117 million, and the trade went down. Griffey went to Cincinnati, which sent four players to the Mariners—center fielder Mike Cameron and pitcher Brett Tomko, plus minor-league pitcher Jake Meyer and infielder Antonio Perez.

Griffey may have left Seattle, but he was never forgotten. For years, Mariners fans would get excited at every rumor that the club might swing a deal to bring Griffey back. The rumors had no substance, but the fans' appreciation for Griffey did.

There's little doubt that if he would come back, even as an opposing player, Seattle fans would welcome Griffey warmly. They gave former pitcher Randy Johnson a long, loud ovation when he returned for the first time to pitch for the Arizona Diamondbacks on July 20, 1999.

"They would give Junior a standing ovation here," former teammate Mike Blowers said. "If they did it for Randy, they surely would do it for Junior."

Until then, all that remain are the memories of what Griffey did for baseball in Seattle. The fans will never release the image of that amazing swing, those leaps into the center-field fence and, above all, the joy he brought to the ballpark.

"He had that ear-to-ear smile," teammate Jay Buhner said. "That smile said everything about his energy and the way he loved the game."

CHAPTER TEN

Turning Losers Into Winners

THE MARINERS BEGAN THE 1991 SEASON believing they finally would put together a winning record. Of course, the M's and their fans had been thinking that for years, and they'd never won more than 78 games.

The talented young Mariners had experienced big-league growing pains in previous seasons, but there was little doubt that this core group of players was capable of winning.

Harold Reynolds was a young second baseman whose speed gave the Mariners a quality leadoff hitter.

Third baseman Edgar Martinez had batted .302 in 1990, his first full major-league season, and was showing qualities of a great right-handed hitter.

Ken Griffey Jr. had batted .300 with 22 home runs and 80 RBIs the previous season and, barring injury, his production could only go up.

DH Alvin Davis was nearing the end of his career, but in the hitter-friendly Kingdome, he remained capable of 15 to 20 home runs and 60 to 70 RBIs.

Jay Buhner, a power-hitting outfielder who played 51 games in 1990, became the Opening-Day starter in right field.

Dave Valle, a quality defensive player behind the plate, returned as the starting catcher.

Journeyman outfielder Tracey Jones started in left field as the Mariners sought stability in a position that had seen four different players there in the previous five years.

The anchor to the defense was Omar Vizquel, the young Venezuelan shortstop who already had displayed his amazing hands in two major-league seasons.

"When Omar started playing every day, it was like, 'Wow!'" pitcher Bill Krueger said. "The kid couldn't hit his way out of a brown paper bag, but oh he could play the field."

On the mound, the Mariners were stout, returning three pitchers from the 1990 rotation who offered unlimited promise—Randy Johnson, Brian Holman, and Erik Hanson.

Johnson had a wild streak—he led the league in walks in 1990—but his dominance became clearly evident. He went 14-11 in 1990, the first winning record of his short career, and finished with five complete games, a 3.65 ERA and 194 strikeouts.

Johnson's biggest conquest was a no-hitter against the Tigers on June 2, 1990, at the Kingdome. It was this performance that illustrated how dominant but also how wild he was early in his career. The Tigers couldn't handle his blazing fastball and knee-buckling slider, but he issued six walks.

Six weeks earlier on a cool night in late April, Brian Holman had silenced the Oakland A's, taking a perfect game into the ninth inning at the Coliseum. He got the first two outs easily, then faced Ken Phelps, the former Mariners first baseman. Phelps jumped on Holman's first pitch, driving it over the fence in right-center field for a home run that ruined the perfect game, the no-hitter and the shutout.

Hanson, a 6-foot-6 right-hander, established himself as a bona-fide starter in 1990 with an 18-6 record and a 3.24 ERA.

Rich DeLucia (who pitched five games after being called up in September) and Bill Krueger (6-8 after 17 starts in 1990 with the Brewers) rounded out the starting rotation.

The 1991 Mariners had more than enough talent to produce a winning record, but they still had to overcome a long-standing feeling that it would take more than talent to win.

"Those guys kept reading and hearing about how hapless or hopeless the Mariners had been," team president Chuck Armstrong

Harold Reynolds smiles from the dugout in 1985. *Photo by The Herald of Everett, WA*

said. "But if you looked at the team position by position, we were better then in a lot of positions than we are today. And it was not a bad starting rotation, especially if you got those guys in a good year. It just shows what a mental game this is."

Manager Jim Lefebvre, an enthusiastic skipper who did his best to instill a winning approach, was beginning his third year, and many players had heard his spiel before.

"Jim, for all his critics, projected a positive image," Krueger said. "You could kind of drink the Kool-Aid with him for a while and it got you fired up. Over time, it wore on some guys, a lot of guys. He'd played for the Dodgers and he was a winner and he wanted to project that on this club and see some things change. We weren't just hoping to win, he projected that we had good players and we were going to win.

"A lot of players were hungry to hear that. The Dave Valles and Harold Reynoldses and Alvin Davises had been through all that losing and they were pretty fed up with it."

The Mariners didn't go into 1991 with aspirations of a championship. When you haven't finished better than .500, there are other goals to achieve first.

"You can't go from last place to winning a world championship all at once," Valle said. "You've got to strive for something that's reachable."

So the Mariners began the 1991 season full of hope, but also with a realistic approach to what they could accomplish. Before anyone dreamed of reaching the postseason, a .500 record was their target.

"For us," Valle said, "that was step No. 1."

Six games into the season, the Mariners took a giant step backward. Both the Angels and A's swept them in two series on the road, and the Mariners returned to the Kingdome for their home opener 0-6.

Despite hearing all the talk about this being a different season, Mariners fans already had a here-we-go-again feeling. Then the M's turned that wicked start around.

"We didn't pitch well on that opening trip," Krueger said. "But you knew that eventually these guys were going to pitch. Once we started pitching, we had a chance to string wins together."

Johnson pitched a complete game and beat the Minnesota Twins 8-4, and the Mariners swept their opening homestand, winning three from the Twins and three from the A's. Then they went back to Anaheim and won the first two games against the Angels.

The Mariners lost seven of their next nine, but followed that stretch with victories in 13 of 15, putting them eight games above .500 on May 20. The streaky nature of the team continued until the All-Star break, with the Mariners enduring stretches when they lost seven straight, won seven of 10, and lost eight of nine. They had a 40-42 record at the break.

After the break, the Mariners won 17 of 23, were nine games above. 500 by August 4 and were playing with a sense of confidence.

"We realized we were capable of playing with anybody," Valle said. "Most of the players were starting to come into their own that year. Junior was coming into his own as a star player. With Randy Johnson, we knew we had a dominating pitcher who gave us a chance to win every fifth day. All of those things colliding at the same time started to make us think, 'We can do this.'"

An early September losing streak dropped the record to 68-69, and the Mariners hovered around the .500 mark heading into the final 10 days of the season. A loss at Chicago on September 28 left them 77-77 with eight games remaining.

After 15 years of losing, the Mariners would either break that stigma or extend it in their final two series of the season, four games at Texas and three at the Kingdome against the White Sox.

Jay Buhner homered in the 11th inning, and the Mariners beat the Rangers 3-2 in the first game of a doubleheader to begin the series at Texas. Krueger pitched well in the second game, holding the Rangers to seven hits in a complete game, but Brian Downing's home run in the first inning and Monty Fariss' homer in the fifth beat the Mariners 2-0.

In the third game of the series, right-hander Dave Burba, making only his second start after spending most of the season either in the bullpen or the minors, held the Rangers to three hits in six innings, and Calvin Jones pitched the final three to finish an 8-1 victory, the Mariners' 80th of the season.

On October 2, the Mariners sent young left-hander Dave Fleming to the mound with a chance to win their 81st game and clinch the first .500 record in franchise history. Fleming held the Rangers to just three hits in 4⅔ innings, but two of those were home runs—a solo shot by Julio Franco in the first inning and a two-run blow by Dean Palmer in the fifth—and Texas took a 3-0 lead.

Then the Mariners came back.

Valle led off the sixth inning with a double and scored when Edgar Martinez doubled. Martinez went to third on Harold Reynolds' ground out, then scored when Rangers right-hander Jose Guzman threw a wild pitch, cutting the Rangers' lead to 3-2.

Manager Jim Lefebvre and catcher Dave Valle talk to pitcher Bill Krueger.
Photo by The Herald of Everett, WA

In the seventh, Buhner singled and Vizquel walked, and Valle drove them both home with a double. The Mariners led 4-3, and their bullpen kept it that way.

Scott Bankhead pitched 2⅓ scoreless innings in relief of Fleming, and Mike Jackson didn't allow a hit in the next 1⅓ innings, striking out Juan Gonzalez for the first out in the ninth inning.

Manager Jim Lefebvre brought in left-hander Russ Swan, who got Kevin Reimer on a grounder back to the mound for the second out.

Lefebvre went to the bullpen again, bringing in right-hander Bill Swift to face Palmer. Swift ended it, getting Palmer to bounce back to the mound for the final out and a historic moment for the Mariners.

To the players who'd endured years of losing, it felt like they'd won the World Series.

"I know a lot of the players didn't realize the historic significance of it, and I use that term—historic—lightly," Valle said. "But for us it was. For myself, Alvin Davis, Harold Reynolds and the others who had been battling for respect in the big leagues, it was a big night for us."

Davis grabbed trainer Rick Griffin and gave him a huge hug.

"We're not losers anymore!" Davis told Griffin.

Valle, who drove in the tying and winning runs, couldn't contain his emotions. During a postgame interview with play-by-play announcer Dave Niehaus, Valle broke down crying.

"I got choked up because I was thinking of everything it had taken for us to get there," Valle said. "We had been the butt of all the jokes for so long. But it was a day for us."

The Mariners won two of their final three games, finishing the season 83-79.

Momentum Lost

Having shed the loser label in 1991, the Mariners had every reason to believe they'd win more games in 1992. Most of the lineup returned, and the club made off-season changes to pump up the offense.

"Those who hadn't been there for all the losing felt good about what we'd done," Krueger said. "But beyond that, this was just like, 'OK, but we expect to win. Now if we can add one hitter, we can go on to the next subject.'"

Instead, the 1992 season turned into a very sore subject.

Jim Lefebvre didn't return as manager, having lost his handle on the clubhouse after three seasons. Players who'd worn "Lefebvre believer" T-shirts three years earlier when he was hired were ready to burn them by the end of the '91 season, despite the team's success.

"To Jim's credit, he had a plan," trainer Rick Griffin said. "When he started, he said we were going to have a winning record, and we did. That's one of the highlights of my career. But there was a lot of uneasiness in the clubhouse and mistrust in the clubhouse. A lot of times, players didn't feel like there was a lot of honesty."

The Mariners promoted Bill Plummer, who had managed the Mariners' Class AAA Calgary team and was a favorite of many young players who developed under him.

They acquired left fielder Kevin Mitchell, the former National League MVP who'd hit 109 home runs and driven in 287 runs the previous three seasons, in a trade with the Giants that ultimately proved costly. Mitchell was a bust, with only nine home runs and 67 RBIs for the Mariners, and certainly not worth the price the Mariners paid to get him—pitchers Bill Swift, Mike Jackson, and Dave Burba.

Swift went 31-12 the next two seasons with the Giants, including 21-8 in 1993. Jackson became one of the game's top closers later in the 1990s, and Burba was a solid member of the Giants' pitching staff both out of the bullpen and as a starter, including a 10-3 record in 1993.

"That trade might have cost us more than 15 wins," Griffin said. "We got a guy who didn't particularly want to play, and we traded away three unbelievably good arms. Those guys all had very good careers."

The Mariners also let longtime fan favorite Alvin Davis flee to free agency (he signed with the Angels) and replaced him with promising young first baseman Tino Martinez, who was their first-round draft pick in 1988.

Randy Johnson, Dave Fleming, and Erik Hanson returned to the starting rotation, but after them, the other two rotation spots were uncertain.

Brian Holman, who came within one out of pitching a perfect game in 1990 and won 13 games in 1991, tore his rotator cuff and never pitched again.

Behind Johnson, Fleming, and Hanson, six other pitchers made the bulk of the remaining starts in 1992—Russ Swan, Brian Fisher, Rich DeLucia, Mark Grant, Tim Leary, and Clay Parker. The Mariners used 23 different pitchers that season.

They lost 13 of 15 games in May and never climbed out of their downward spiral, finishing 64-98.

Plummer struggled as well in his first, and only, season as manager.

Early in the season, he filled out the lineup card with two first basemen and no DH for a game at Chicago in mid-April. The Mariners made numerous lineup changes to avoid having the pitchers hit, and they lost 5-4 to the White Sox.

At times as the season wore on, Plummer seemed indifferent to what was happening.

"When he'd walk back from the mound after a pitching change, he'd look into the stands and shrug his shoulders as if to say, 'Hey, it's not my fault,'" said Jim Street, who covered the Mariners for the *Seattle Post-Intelligencer.*

On the final day of the season, Plummer and Griffey got into an argument on the bench after Griffey had thought he would play only a few innings. Instead, Plummer left him in for six innings and three at-bats.

"Junior played with his shoelaces untied, he was so upset. He even made a catch over his head with his shoelaces untied," said John Moses, who replaced Griffey in the seventh inning. "He thought he was only going to get an at-bat and that was it, but Plum left him in until the seventh."

A new skipper was in place the next year, and it became the best hire in franchise history.

CHAPTER ELEVEN

Lou Piniella:

THE MAN WHO BROUGHT A PASSION TO WIN

THE MARINERS THOUGHT THEY KNEW LOU PINIELLA.

He's the guy who never hesitated to jump in an umpire's face, the guy who wrestled with Rob Dibble in the Cincinnati clubhouse, the guy who managed the Reds to the 1990 World Series title, the guy who'd been hired and fired by George Steinbrenner.

In 1993, when Piniella became the 11th manager of the Mariners, they thought they knew what he was all about because they'd known his record of excellence and seen his greatest fits.

They didn't know the half of Lou Piniella.

"Lou is one of the great characters in baseball," said John McLaren, a coach on Piniella's teams in Cincinnati, Seattle, and Tampa Bay. "He's a little bit George Steinbrenner, a little bit Billy Martin, and a little bit Casey Stengel."

Piniella could melt a person with the twinkle in his eye and a funny story, but he also could stare daggers through a young player when he was angry. He was famous for his tirades with umpires, and he had one of his best with the Mariners in 1998 when he kicked his cap across the diamond in Cleveland.

The young Mariners of 1993 didn't realize how deep Piniella's passion ran.

They didn't know that his tender heart and compassion for his fellow man would bring tears to his eyes.

Manager Lou Piniella shouts directions to the infield in 1997.
Photo by Dan Bates/The Herald of Everett, WA

They had no idea how much Piniella loved to win and how badly he hated to lose. Any loss, at any time or anywhere, was more than he could stomach.

"As far as I'm concerned, everything we accomplished in 1995 started in 1993 when Lou came here," said Mike Blowers, who was a 28-year-old third baseman on that team.

When Piniella addressed the Mariners on the first day of spring training in 1993, he made it clear that the attitude of the club would be different, and that the losing mind-set that had prevailed in previous years was going to stop.

"He expected to win every day, and that included spring training," Blowers said. "The amount of intensity he brought every day and his expectations of us were tremendous. All the guys who were able to survive that spring and make the club and make it through a season had a real appreciation for what Lou was all about.

"We might lose a game on a Tuesday night in Detroit in mid-July, when it might seem like nobody really cared, but that man was sick to his stomach over it. It was awesome."

When the Mariners lost a couple of games in a row, Piniella might not shave. Another loss or two, and he wouldn't comb his hair.

"If it continued he might not even button his shirt," trainer Rick Griffin said. "He'd be so mad thinking about the games, he didn't care if he looked like a hobo."

No Time for Losing...Or Losers

There's no such thing as a meaningless game to Lou Piniella, whether it's a spring training exhibition or a midweek game in the dog days of summer.

That much was evident when he was managing the Cincinnati Reds in 1992 during a March exhibition game against the Detroit Tigers. Actor Tom Selleck, a lifelong Tigers fan, suited up for the game and got an at-bat. He was doing well, too, fouling off several curveballs from Reds pitcher Tim Layana to stay alive at the plate.

Piniella, however, was in the dugout fuming.

"He fouled off four or five, and Lou was ticked," coach John McLaren said. "Finally, Lou says, 'Throw him the heater and get him the hell out of there.'"

Layana did and Selleck struck out.

"I've never seen anybody so consumed with winning and what it takes to win as Lou," McLaren said. "That's all he's about. There are no false pretenses whatsoever."

Oh, did those 1993 Seattle Mariners learn all about that.

Charged with turning around a team that had won just 64 games in 1992, Piniella's first spring training was stressful. The Mariners played every exhibition game on the road in '93 because the new stadium at their spring training complex in Peoria, Arizona, was still a year away from being ready.

"They won a few games right away that spring, and I remember Lou wondering how that team could possibly have lost 98 games the previous year," said Larry LaRue, who covers the Mariners for *The News Tribune* of Tacoma.

Then the Mariners went on a horrible losing streak.

"It wasn't long before Lou was wondering how they ever won 64," LaRue said.

After one spring training loss, Piniella ordered the team bus to pull over when he saw a couple of youth teams playing on a field near the road. Then he railed on the Mariners, saying he doubted they could beat those kids.

"After the first 10 games of spring training, I told Sammy Ellis, our pitching coach, 'Hell with taking me to the next ballpark. Get me to the airport. I'm going to fly home in my uniform,'" Piniella said. "It was that bad, but we got it turned around and played about .500 that spring and then we played over .500 the first year here."

Piniella has played to win ever since he was a kid in Tampa. He played in the Indians and Orioles minor-league systems in the mid-1960s and he was the Seattle Pilots' 28th pick in baseball's 1968 expansion draft. Piniella never played for the Pilots, who traded him to the Royals just before the 1969 season opener. In Kansas City, he batted .282 and won the American League Rookie of the Year award, and built his reputation as a fiery, 110-percent-effort player. He played his final 11 seasons with that same intensity with the Yankees.

When he became a manager, Piniella was no different.

George Steinbrenner hired him to manage the Yankees in 1986, and Piniella won 90 and 89 games his first two seasons. The Yankees never finished higher than second and, riding in fifth place after 93 games in 1988, Steinbrenner fired Piniella.

The Reds hired him in 1990 and he turned a team of budding young players—the Reds' roster averaged 27.5 years—into World Series champions, sweeping Oakland in four games.

Piniella managed two more years in Cincinnati, then came to Seattle and inherited a team much like the young Reds. The Mariners' roster averaged 28 years and they needed the direction of a fiery leader who didn't accept losing.

"Ever since I played against Lou in the mid-'60s, he had an insatiable desire to win," said Lee Elia, Piniella's hitting coach with the Mariners. "He couldn't stand mediocrity. Lou expected a person to play as good as God gave him the ability to play, and anything less would be a failure. That fed into the clubhouse. The players knew that when they crossed the lines, they'd better bust their asses because they'd have to face Lou if they didn't. He didn't really care about the peripherals."

Even the 2001 Mariners, who tied the all-time major-league record with 116 victories, stressed Piniella when they lost. That team lost three in a row only once all season.

"If you didn't know during that season that we were such a great team, you'd have thought we were 15 games out of first place by looking at Lou," trainer Rick Griffin said. "He pushed those guys and never backed off."

Piniella and the Young Ballplayer

Bret Boone, the Mariners' fifth-round draft choice in 1990, was determined to make an impression on Lou Piniella as he began spring training in 1993. He got that chance in the first at-bat of his first exhibition game, stepping to the plate with nobody out and a runner on second base against the Angels, ready to make an impact.

"I was a confident young player and I wanted to show the new skipper what I could do," Boone said. "But Chuck Finley was on the mound and he had that nasty split-finger. I knew I had to get the runner over to third, and Finley threw me a first-pitch fastball but I fouled it into the first-base dugout."

Finley threw a splitter on the next pitch and it fooled Boone, who lunged onto his front foot. Still, he made solid contact and smoked the ball down the third-base line, a sure double that would drive in a run, Boone thought. However, Angels third baseman Gary Gaetti made a diving catch, then threw to second base to turn what seemed like a moment of glory for Boone into a double play.

Boone figured he'd scored a few positive points with Piniella for hitting the ball so hard.

"I'm coming back to the dugout with my chest puffed out a little, thinking to myself, 'Man, I hit that ball hard. Skip's going to be happy with me,'" Boone said.

He descended the dugout steps, getting high-fives from teammates, when Piniella met him.

"Son," Piniella began, "you really knocked the crap out of that ball."

Anyone who'd been around Piniella, even for only a short while, knew that when he addressed a person "son," it wasn't a warm, fatherly greeting.

Lou Piniella challenged Bret Boone and helped make him into a valuable player for the Mariners. *Photo by Stephanie S. Cordle/The Herald of Everett, WA*

"Son," Piniella said again to Boone. "You made no attempt to move the runner over. Now get out of here and get your running in."

Boone was perplexed.

"Is he kidding? Did he just take me out of the game after one at-bat?" Boone wondered. "No, he's not kidding."

So Boone took off his spikes, pulled on his running shoes and began his conditioning work by running along the outfield warning track as the game went on.

"Here I was in the first inning of my first game with the new skipper, and I'm out there not knowing what to think," Boone said. "The crowd out there was really getting on me for it."

That exchange sent a clear signal to the team what Piniella was all about, coach John McLaren said.

"He's all about the team concept and that individual baseball wasn't going to cut it," McLaren said. "He sent a strong message right there."

And Piniella kept sending it. He rode Boone throughout spring training, and Boone endured it with one thought.

"The guy hates me," he said. "It turned out that he didn't hate me at all. He was testing me. Lou is not for the faint at heart. My first year, Lou and I had some drag-out arguments. I was going to be respectful, but I was trying to establish myself as a major-league player and I was going to tell him what I thought."

Piniella's tirades with young players may have seemed personal and unfair, but McLaren said he challenged them for the right reasons. Piniella, in fact, enjoyed those who stood up for themselves in the face of his criticism.

"I would always tell a young player, 'You will be challenged by Lou,'" McLaren said. "'If you defend your turf and come back at Lou in a respectful, professional way, you will never have a problem with him.'"

In the mid-1990s, young pitcher Ken Cloude was struggling during one game, and Piniella sent his pitching coach, Nardi Contreras, to the mound.

After a brief talk with Cloude, Contreras walked back to the dugout with a smile on his face.

"What's so funny?" Piniella asked.

"Skip, I asked the kid, 'Can you get this guy out?'" Contreras told Piniella. "And he said, 'I can if you get your ass off the mound.'"

Piniella loved that kind of attitude from his players.

"If you came back at Lou and were positive in your thinking and you showed strength, you never had a problem," McLaren said. "But there were guys who were intimidated by Lou."

Catcher Dan Wilson was one of those early in his career, McLaren said. Wilson, a former first-round draft pick of the Reds who had caught Piniella's eye there, came to the Mariners after the

1993 season, along with relief pitcher Bobby Ayala, in exchange for Boone and pitcher Erik Hanson.

Wilson was by no means soft, but he was a quiet, respectful 25-year-old who absorbed all of what Piniella dished to him. McLaren begged Wilson not to take that from Piniella, to speak back.

"But I respect the man so much," Wilson told McLaren.

"That's fine, Danny, but you've got to defend yourself a little bit," McLaren told him. "He has challenged every catcher who's ever played for him and he's going to challenge you, and if you don't defend your turf, you're in for a long, tough ride."

Wilson survived and became one of Piniella's favorite players in the nine seasons he managed the Mariners.

"Lou either made them good players or he cracked them. He made men," coach Lee Elia said. "Dan Wilson's first year here was very difficult. If something went wrong, it was always Danny's fault. Lou would ask him, 'Why did you throw that pitch? Where was it?' Danny was strong enough inside to never blame a pitcher. He would take the brunt of it. But through that, Danny gained more strength.

"There were other guys like that. If he stayed on their ass, they either grew up or he cracked them. At that time, we started to develop some men."

Piniella challenged his players because he wanted to learn who he could depend on in tense, game-winning situations and who he couldn't. He wasn't interested in the weak or tentative player; he wanted a player who competed to win every minute of every game.

"I've seen him be very tough on people," Boone said. "I don't know if I always agreed with it, but that's his way. I love the guy."

Many of the players who flourished under Piniella were the ones he rode the hardest.

"He was hard on people, but I thought he was extremely fair," third baseman Mike Blowers said. "When he chewed my butt out, I usually deserved it."

Not every player understood Piniella like that.

Pitcher Mike Schooler saved 63 games for the Mariners in the 1989 and 1990 seasons, but arm injuries derailed one of the game's best closers, and he was never the same. Schooler's ERA climbed, his save totals went down and, midway through spring training in 1993, the Mariners released him.

"That Piniella," Schooler told reporters after the club let him go. "All he cares about is winning."

Laughing with Lou

Lou Piniella's intensity often brought smiles to the Mariners' faces.

"He's an in-your-face kind of guy, but he's got a funny way of loosening guys up," outfielder Jay Buhner said. "And it was inevitable that he would do something that was bone-headed."

During one game in Kansas City, Piniella got so upset that he vented his anger on the dugout water cooler.

"He was beating up on it, picking it up and tossing it down," Buhner said. "Then he hauled off and kicked it so hard that he ripped his toenail off. He's there yelling, 'Aww, my mother f---ing toe!' But we're all laughing about it."

Buhner remembers how the late umpire Durwood Merrill would bait Piniella because he enjoyed watching Piniella's antics. During a game at Minnesota, Piniella snapped and, after arguing with Merrill, tried to pull third base from its peg so he could throw it. The bag wouldn't budge.

"Lou's trying to get the bag out of the ground and it's not coming," Buhner said. "He's yanking and yanking, and finally he says, 'Aw, f--- it!' The next day, I show up at the ballpark and there's Lou on the training table. He'd blown his back out."

Piniella had a few base-throwing moments, but his most volatile tirade occurred in 1998 in Cleveland. He became so incensed that he flung his cap while arguing in shallow left field, then kicked it all the way back to the dugout. On the Mariners' bench, Ken Griffey Jr. covered his face with his glove to hide his uncontrollable laughter.

"Some of the stuff Lou did would make us want to flat-out roar, but we always had to hold back," said Lee Elia, Piniella's former hitting coach. "One day he was on the bench flipping a ball. He'd flip it up and catch it, flip it up and catch it. Then he flipped it up and it never came back down. He had flipped it over the dugout roof, but he didn't realize that right away. We were watching him out of the corner of our eye, and he was wondering how that ball just disappeared. His expression was priceless."

Piniella rarely made a trip to the mound without his zig-zag walk, his mind focused more on the game than the route from the dugout.

"He would swagger out there, say a sentence to the pitcher and walk back," Elia said. "Then he'd get about three-quarters of the way back and look up, and the dugout would be way over there."

Piniella's patience nearly ran dry in 1995 when the major leaguers were on strike and spring training camps were filled with replacement players. One pop-fly drill became such a disaster that Piniella called it off before someone got hurt.

"That's when the word 'rumdum' came into his vocabulary," coach John McLaren said.

Piniella the Mastermind

Lou Piniella was at his best running a game. He always seemed to be a step ahead of the opposing manager, and his own players were amazed at his knowledge of their strengths and weaknesses, and how he could use them to the Mariners' advantage.

"Everybody looks for the lefty-righty matchup, but Lou was the only manager I'd ever seen who would take into consideration what a pitcher threw," third baseman Mike Blowers said.

During one game, Blowers was on the bench sitting next to Piniella when the other team brought in a right-handed relief pitcher. Piniella turned to Blowers, a right-handed hitter, and said, "It defied baseball logic, and Blowers didn't get it."

Blowers didn't get it.

"He throws a sinker and you're a good low-ball hitter," Piniella told Blowers. "You can hit this guy."

Blowers got a hit.

"I always felt we had an advantage because Lou was in our dugout," Blowers said. "He knew the other teams' hitters, and he knew their pitchers. He was better than any scouting report. He knew how to position a defense, what to throw a guy, how to use the bench. He pushed every right button he possibly could, and it wasn't by accident or luck."

Piniella's best managerial performance may have been the 1995 season, when the Mariners surged from 13 games behind the Angels to win the American League West title.

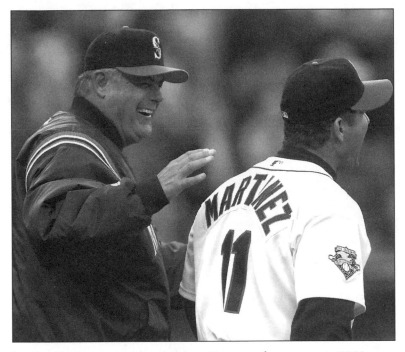

Lou Piniella shares a laugh with Edgar Martinez after a game in 2001.
Photo by Stephanie S. Cordle/The Herald of Everett, WA

"From the middle of August until that season was over, he was so focused on what the job for each night was," coach Lee Elia said. "It was almost like he was in a trance. Nothing overwhelmed him and every move was the right move.

"When we played the Yankees in the first round, Lou knew Joe Torre and his players, and he could feel every move they were going to make and he was ready to counter them. Lou always made a pitching change in a situation where they couldn't counter with a pinch hitter. He always had the right matchups, whether it was offensive or pitching. It was unbelievable how sharp Lou was in that six-week timeframe. We all marveled at it. He was brilliant."

A Man of Compassion

As hard as he was on players and umpires, Lou Piniella often showed a tender heart.

Before every season opener, Piniella would make his way around the clubhouse, giving every player a handshake and a hug.

"Some of the guys he'd had cantankerous relationships with, but it didn't matter," pitching coach Bryan Price said. "He was very fatherly to the players."

"I was intimidated by him at first because I used to see him from the other side," said Mike Cameron, who played for the Mariners from 2000 to 2003. "But once you get to know him, you realize he's one of the most caring people you could possibly meet."

Nothing revealed Piniella's heart more than an evening in Chicago when the Mariners, after losing a tough game, arrived at their hotel. Outside the lobby, a desperate young woman pleaded for help.

"Fellas, this is awkward for me," she said. "I've never done this before, but I'm broke and my kids are at home and they're hungry. I'm not asking for a dime or a dollar. Do you have twenty?"

"You seem sincere about this," Piniella told her.

"I'm very sincere, sir. I just lost my job, I don't have a husband and I've got two kids at home. One is so small I've got to use formula to feed him but I don't have any money for it."

Piniella turned to Lee Elia, his hitting coach, and said, "Lee, go inside and ask where the closest grocery store is."

Elia did, and then he, Piniella and the woman jumped in a cab and rode to the store. Piniella bought baby formula, diapers and groceries. The bill was more than $300, and Piniella paid it. He helped load the groceries into the cab and, as the woman climbed into the back seat, he gave the driver a $20 and told him to get her home safely.

Neither Piniella nor Elia said much during their walk back to the hotel.

Elia looked at Piniella and saw tears in his eyes.

"Lou?" Elia asked. "You all right?"

"Dammit, Lee," Piniella said. "I don't know if I got her enough stuff."

CHAPTER TWELVE

Poised for a Championship

THE SEEDS OF THE MARINERS' GREAT TEAMS of the mid-1990s and beyond were planted in the '80s with good drafts and effective trades. Center fielder Ken Griffey Jr. and DH Edgar Martinez developed through the Mariners' minor-league system. Right fielder Jay Buhner, catcher Dan Wilson, and pitcher Randy Johnson arrived through trades.

Those players led the Mariners to their first division championship in 1995 and set a standard for those who followed them. Under Lou Piniella's direction, the Mariners changed the way fans in Seattle and all of baseball viewed the franchise. They were no longer an American League outpost that was largely ignored and hardly appreciated.

In the mid-1990s, the Mariners matured into a team capable of beating anyone, anywhere, and, in addition to Griffey, those four players—Johnson, Martinez, Buhner, and Wilson—were the foundation.

Randy Johnson:
A Talk With the Master, Then Dominance

A baseball philosopher once said, "Show me a player with potential, and I'll show you a guy who hasn't done squat."

After three and a half seasons with the Mariners, Randy Johnson hadn't done squat. He'd come to the Mariners in a trade with the Montreal Expos in 1989, and in 119 starts with the M's, Johnson put together a mediocre record of 46-44.

He was a gangly-looking, walk-an-inning machine who struggled to get all the parts of his 6-foot-10 body in sync. The result was the American League lead in walks for three straight seasons and hit batters in two of them. He walked 120 and hit 12 in 1990, walked 152 and hit 18 in 1991, and walked 144 and hit 16 in 1992.

With a 100-mph fastball, a slider that froze hitters at the plate, and sometimes no idea where those pitches were headed, Johnson was an every-fifth-day enigma early in his career. The good Randy was almost unhittable; the wild Randy struggled to throw strikes. He'd walk 10 in a game one start, then flirt with a no-hitter in another.

"He was elbows and kneecaps and came at you with maximum effort," said Bill Krueger, a teammate on the 1991 club who became a friend of Johnson's. "He was a roller coaster on the field, but you could definitely see the greatness coming. He lived at 100 mph for the first three or four innings, and this wasn't 100 mph that was pumped up by a false radar gun reading like we see at the ballparks today. This was Nolan Ryan 100."

The good Randy and the wild Randy converged for the biggest night in Mariners history on June 2, 1990. He walked six and pitched a no-hitter against the Detroit Tigers—the first in the history of the Mariners (Chris Bosio has the only other, on April 23, 1993).

Pitching coaches worked with Johnson to corral his control issues, and he was tireless in his own preparation. Only time, it seemed, would allow his body to catch up with that golden arm and produce the consistency needed to become a great pitcher.

The key to Johnson's transformation, strangely, may have been a series of celebrity blackjack tournaments that trainer Rick Griffin entered. He struck up a friendship with Nolan Ryan after a tournament in 1991.

Griffin told Ryan about the issues Johnson was facing, and he asked if Ryan might be able to talk with him when the Mariners played at Texas during the 1992 season. Ryan said he'd be glad to

Randy Johnson (left) and Nolan Ryan shake hands during pregame warmups.
Photo courtesy of the Seattle Mariners

and, on the Mariners' first trip there in June, he didn't forget his promise.

"Bring him over and we can talk for about 15 minutes," he told Griffin.

Griffin introduced Johnson to Ryan about 6:15 p.m. and went back to the Mariners' clubhouse to prepare for the game, which started about 7.

"They were only going to talk for 15 minutes, but Randy didn't come back to our clubhouse until the fourth inning," Griffin said.

"It was about eight o'clock, and he'd been talking with Nolan all that time."

Ryan told Johnson about his off-day throwing program, and how he doesn't always throw off the mound between starts in order to take the stress off his arm. They talked about how much Ryan runs and lifts between starts. They talked about pitching mechanics, and Ryan said he'd noticed Johnson landing on his heel instead of the ball of his right foot when he delivered a pitch.

"Randy started doing all that stuff they talked about, and all of a sudden he just took off," Griffin said. "That was a turning point."

The following season, Johnson's walks went down and his strikeouts went up. Johnson went 19-8 the next season and pitched an impressive 255⅓ innings.

He became the cornerstone of the Mariners' rise to their first division championship. He won 13 games in the strike-shortened 1994 season, then went 18-2 with a league-best 2.48 earned run average and won the American League Cy Young Award in 1995, when the Mariners made their incredible late-season surge to win the American League West title.

"If we'd lost three or four in a row, the Unit would pitch and he would stop the streak," said Lee Elia, the hitting coach under manager Lou Piniella in the mid-1990s. "And if we'd won four or five in a row, the Unit would keep it going for another four or five."

That once-erratic left-hander also shucked his wild side, never again walking more than 99 in a season. He still hit batters, but that could have been as much intimidation as wildness.

Yes, Johnson got into the heads of hitters.

"He's the most fiercely competitive person I know," Griffin said. "He will intimidate you and do what he's got to do in order to win. He brings the same intensity to a baseball game that you would find in a football player."

That intensity would begin long before Johnson took the mound. For a whole day before his starts, it was best to avoid him. Henry Genzale, the Mariners' clubhouse manager, once asked Johnson—on the day he was to pitch—if he needed a new pair of socks.

"It's not my day to talk," Johnson barked. "Don't bother me."

There was another incident when the Mariners were on a cross-country flight. Johnson, who'd had a tough day, was in the back of the plane playing cards when a flight attendant spilled a drink on him.

"Randy got pissed, stood up and hit his head on a bulkhead," Krueger said. "That really set him off and he came storming up the aisle, then he punched the emergency exit sign right off the ceiling of the plane. For a while we thought we would have to make an emergency landing, but it turned out one of the crew on the plane knew how to fix it."

Johnson, never the best-liked ballplayer, had run-ins with the media and conflicts with teammates, including one that escalated into a clubhouse fight in 1998. Johnson became upset when Mariners teammate David Segui turned up the volume on the clubhouse stereo. The confrontation got physical, and media reports said Segui shoved Johnson into his locker. Segui suffered a sprained right wrist and missed a game.

When reporters asked Segui how he was injured, he wasn't apologetic.

"I hurt it on a 6-foot-10 piece of sh--," Segui said.

Maybe some teammates had that opinion of Johnson, but it was far from universal. Krueger got to know him as a good person who worried about things he shouldn't have.

"He be asking, 'How many walks do I have?' and 'Where's my ERA now?'" Krueger said. "He could be a pain in the ass. Some days when Randy was in a bad mood, he could brush you off with the best of them.

"But Randy has a good heart. He cares about other people. A lot of things happened in his life. He was self-absorbed to a degree and some of that changed. His father passing was a huge blow in his life and to meet (his wife) Lisa in a short window of time changed his life. His priorities changed and he was able to direct his energy and commitment and the rage that was inside of him to become a great pitcher."

As the years went by, Johnson felt less and less appreciated by the Mariners. He'd never gotten over an incident before the 1993 season when he was in the team offices just after the Christmas break. Team president Chuck Armstrong innocently asked Johnson how his holidays had been. Unknown to Armstrong, Johnson's father had died of an aneurism during the holidays.

Johnson's relationship with the Mariners soured significantly in 1998 when the club refused to offer a contract extension beyond that year. He became a frequent subject of trade rumors and grew tired of the increasing number of questions about his future.

Johnson, a 20-game winner in 1997, was just 9-10 after 23 starts in '98 and the widespread speculation was that he had intentionally tanked the season. Those who knew Johnson well believed he took just as much desire to the mound as always, but the distraction over his future undermined his effort to win.

Just minutes before the July 31 trade deadline, Mariners general manager Woody Woodward completed a deal with the Houston Astros, who needed pitching help to make a late-season push in their division. The Mariners got two of the Astros' top minor-league prospects, pitcher Freddy Garcia and shortstop Carlos Guillen, plus a player to be named later (pitcher John Halama).

With the Astros, Johnson was nearly unbeatable the rest of the season. He made 11 more starts, going 10-1 with a 1.48 ERA. The sudden surge to Johnson's old form further infuriated Mariners fans who believed he gave up on the club in his final Seattle season.

"A lot of people, for whatever reason, don't like him, they don't understand him or they choose to think he's a terrible guy," Griffin said. "Randy is an extremely complex individual who nobody is gong to completely figure out. But I've been here for 24 years, and he's one of my favorites."

Edgar Martinez: The Game's Greatest DH

Benny Looper, the Mariners' longtime director of player development, has a personal policy when it comes to handling minor leaguers: Never give up on a kid after one season, no matter how badly he struggles.

In 1983, the Mariners had a 20-year-old from Puerto Rico who struggled like few who'd ever made it beyond the Class-A level. Edgar Martinez batted .173 that year for the Bellingham Mariners, getting 18 hits in 104 at-bats, with just two extra-base hits.

Martinez was worried.

Edgar Martinez. *Photo by Joe Nicholson/The Herald of Everett, WA*

"Every year that I played since Little League, I was the best hitter on the team," he said. "In all the leagues I played, I was the batting champion of the team or the best player. Then I got to Bellingham, and I was shocked that I couldn't hit. I was concerned, but deep down I knew that I could hit."

Martinez did hit, and it didn't take him much longer to get started. He batted .303 the next year at Wausau, when he showed his first signs of power with 15 home runs and 66 RBIs.

Three years later, in 1987, Martinez batted .329 at Triple-A Calgary and earned a September call-up to the Mariners. The next year, back at Calgary, he led the Pacific Coast League with a .363 average.

"That was the first time that I thought I could play in the big leagues," he said. "I remember thinking that what I was doing there, I could do in the big leagues. I knew I could hit."

By 1989, Martinez was the Mariners' starting third baseman and on his way to becoming one of baseball's all-time best right-handed hitters. Over 18 seasons, he won batting championships in 1992 and 1995, played in seven All-Star Games and finished his career with 2,247 hits, a .313 batting average, .418 on-base percentage, and .515 slugging percentage.

No at-bat is remembered as fondly as the moment Martinez dug into the batter's box in the 11th inning at the Kingdome on October 8, 1995. The Mariners trailed the New York Yankees 5-4 in the fifth and deciding game of the American League Division Series, and Martinez came to bat with Joey Cora on third base and Ken Griffey Jr. on first with nobody out.

Facing Yankees right-hander Jack McDowell, Martinez stroked a line drive into the left-field corner, scoring both Cora and Griffey to beat the Yankees 6-5 and send the Mariners into the American League Championship Series against the Cleveland Indians.

"The Double," as it's called, is considered the best moment in Seattle sports history.

"I've seen the replay of that so many times, that is the picture of it that's in my mind now," Martinez said. "I remember going to the plate thinking of it as just another at-bat. A very important at-bat, though."

Get this: Martinez says it wasn't the biggest performance of his career.

That occurred the previous night, when the Yankees jumped to a 5-0 lead over the Mariners and seemed on their way to clinching the series. Then, in one of the great individual performances in postseason history, Martinez took over.

He hit a three-run homer in the third inning to cut the Yankees' lead to 5-3, then belted a grand slam off John Wetteland in the eighth inning to put the Mariners ahead 10-6 in a game they won 11-8.

"I see that game as the biggest in my career, because we had to come from so far behind in such a critical game," Martinez said.

He was the first player in postseason history to drive home seven runs in a game and finished with a .521 average in the series.

For all Martinez did with the bat, he was a leader in the clubhouse who made those around him better players. Bret Boone credits Martinez with helping restore his career in 2001.

Boone had batted over .300 only once in his career, .320 with the Reds in 1994, but wanted badly to resurrect his stroke after signing with the Mariners as a free agent before the 2001 season. He remembers a talk with Martinez at spring training that changed his approach to hitting.

"I know I can hit .280 and drive in 90 runs and hit 20 home runs," Boone told Martinez. "But I can do better than that. I want to hit .300."

"Why are you settling for .300?" Martinez told him. "Why not aim for .340?"

"But my career average says I'm a .280 hitter," Boone said. "Although I did hit .320 one year."

"Does that mean you can't do it again?" Martinez asked. "You should shoot for .340."

The discussion got deeper, delving into the mental approach to hitting and how Martinez separated his thought process from the mechanical aspects of his swing.

Boone went on to have the best season of his career, batting .331 with 37 home runs and 141 RBIs.

"That was a big turning point for me," Boone said. "I came with a lot of experience and I was in the best shape of my life, and I had one of the greatest hitters of our era at my side to pick his brain. Edgar didn't have the natural ability of guys like Barry Bonds or Ken Griffey Jr., but he was a gifted hitter, and he was one of the greatest players I'd ever seen in his heyday."

Jay Buhner: Power at the Plate, Strength in the Clubhouse

In right field, nobody had a stronger arm than Jay Buhner. At the plate, when he'd get on a hot streak, no ballpark could contain him for weeks at a time. In the clubhouse, no Mariner was so instrumental in instilling the desire, confidence, and work ethic to get the most out of his teammates as Buhner.

The Mariners of the mid- and late 1990s featured some of the game's all-time greats—Ken Griffey Jr., Randy Johnson, Edgar Martinez, Alex Rodriguez, Lou Piniella—and they won division championships in 1995 and 1997. One by one, the stars left Seattle. But even though Johnson, Griffey, and Rodriguez were gone, the

Mariners continued to play well and reached the playoffs in 2000 and 2001. A common thread to all those teams was Buhner.

He brought a passion to the clubhouse. He made himself accountable; he made his teammates accountable. He would chew them out, then take them to dinner.

"Jay would get in guys' faces, in the clubhouse or on the bench," said trainer Rick Griffin, who became one of Buhner's best friends. "He would say, 'What are you doing? That's now how you play ball. That's not how you win.' Nobody ever challenged Jay."

At the same time, Buhner was a friend who everybody cherished.

"Jay was the most generous player I've seen in my life," Griffin said. "For seven or eight years, every time we went into another city after a day game, he would grab the young players and some of the veterans, eight or 10 guys, and he would take them to dinner at a nice restaurant. And I mean a nice restaurant, and he would pay for it every time. They would offer to pay and he wouldn't let them. Do that 10 or 15 times a year for seven or eight years, that's a lot of money."

Buhner always considered the reward was so much greater than the expense. At those dinners, the players would talk baseball.

"What can we do to get better?" he would ask his teammates. "What can we do to win? We're facing the Red Sox the next three days, so how do we beat them?"

Buhner learned that when he was a rookie with the Yankees, when Don Mattingly and the veterans would take the young players to dinner and imprint them with the mark of a winner.

He played his first major-league game with the Yankees on September 11, 1987, but came to the Mariners the following July in a trade that sent slugging first baseman Ken Phelps to New York. The trade was a blessing to the Mariners.

Buhner's best years were 1995, '96 and '97, when he hit at least 40 home runs and drove in 100 runs each time. During that three-year stretch, he hit 124 homers and drove in 368, and in 1996 Buhner finally was rewarded for his defense with a Gold Glove. It wasn't a coincidence that the Mariners won two division championships during Buhner's most productive years.

"Those were fun years because we were having fun and winning games," Buhner said. "It was a blast, getting a chance to come into

Jay Buhner hits a home run in 2001. *Photo by Stephanie S. Cordle/The Herald of Everett, WA*

my own, putting up some power numbers and being surrounded by a great group of guys."

Buhner also established a record of injuries that no Mariner may beat. His hard-charging style was hell on his wrists, elbows, shoulders, ankles, knees, and feet. Griffin has a human anatomy chart in the training room at Safeco Field, and during one off-season he decided to log all of Buhner's injuries on it. There were 89.

"The players now come in and see that and think, 'There's no way somebody could have that many injuries and still play,'" Griffin said.

Probably the strangest injury occurred after a game when Buhner was wrestling with a tape cutter, trying to free his heavily wrapped ankle. The cutter slipped and Buhner stabbed himself in the forehead.

With Buhner around, the Mariners played hard, won a lot of games and had as much fun off the field as they did on it. Buhner was a master prankster, and the ruder and cruder, the better.

Former pitching coach Mike Paul would spend considerable time with his hair after games, and Buhner occasionally slipped into the bathroom and sprinkled baby powder inside the blow dryer before Paul got out of the shower.

Buhner could vomit on command—he called it "blurping"—and he typically targeted rookies and others with weak stomachs, particularly manager Lou Piniella.

"Our coaches would come up to me like once a week and say, 'Go get Lou again,'" Buhner said. "So I'd drink some milk and get it to come back up. Then we'd watch Lou tear up and gag. One time he ran into the training room and threw up all over the training table."

Nobody escaped Buhner's blurps, and more than just Piniella lost their lunch because of him.

"There was a day in Anaheim when we had three piles of puke to clean up," Griffin said.

Buhner also established a tradition of making sure the shampoo and conditioner bottles were "filled" after every Mariners road series.

"Always on getaway day no matter where we were at, when we would leave a ballpark I'd always top them off," he said. "I'd usually have a couple bottles of water and a few beers in me."

Buhner would wait until everyone else had showered to make sure he didn't mess with any of his teammates, then leave his "gift" for the next team.

"One time in Detroit I was doing it when Norm Charlton, my partner in crime, started whistling at me," Buhner said. "He was trying to tell me that Lou was coming."

Buhner didn't realize that Piniella hadn't yet showered. When the skipper walked in, he saw Buhner hovering over a shampoo bottle.

"Jesus Christ, Jay. What the hell's going on?" Piniella barked.

"Oh, hey Lou," Buhner said. "Uh, nothing."

Piniella soon figured it out. "Just tell me which ones are safe," he said.

Buhner did.

"All right," Piniella said. "Continue."

Buhner also had a bitter side, particularly toward former manager Jim Lefebvre. The two feuded often, going back to 1989.

"I thought I'd made the team out of spring training," Buhner said. "I led the team in RBIs and home runs, and in the last game I'd gone deep to win a game against Rick Sutcliffe when he was with Chicago. Then I got off the bus and was told I'd been sent down. Jim basically told me to my face that he was going to screw me. Well, what goes around comes around. Mark my word, I was going to have the last laugh."

Lefebvre sent Buhner back to Triple-A and left him there, then often told reporters early that season how the Mariners, who were struggling below .500, could use a right-handed power hitter. Eventually, there was no choice but to call up Buhner, which the Mariners did in June.

"He got his hand forced," Buhner said of Lefebvre. "And even then, he would call me into his office every day and tell me I'd better step up or it would be my last game."

In his fourth game, on June 5 against the Kansas City Royals in the Kingdome, Buhner stepped up to Lefebvre's challenge. He hit a ninth-inning home run to tie the score 3-3, then began a home-run-trot tradition that he continued the rest of his career. As Buhner crossed home plate, he touched the bill of his helmet with his middle finger, looking toward Lefebvre in the dugout.

For the rest of Buhner's career, he touched his helmet with both hands as he crossed the plate after home runs.

"I got rid of the middle finger deal—I can't say I'm proud of that—but it was my way of tipping my hat to him," Buhner said. "As far as I'm concerned, I did get the last laugh."

The Buhner-Lefebvre feud nearly came to blows during a game in 1991 when the manager pulled Buhner out of the on-deck circle and inserted a pinch hitter late in a close game. There was an open area behind the Mariners' dugout in the Kingdome, and Buhner took his bat back there.

"All you could hear was 'Ka-bang! Ka-bang! Ka-bang!'" said pitcher Bill Krueger. "Jay was back there, right behind the part of the dugout where Lefebvre sat, banging on that wall as hard as he could."

Lefebvre went back there and, according to media reports, teammates had to hold Buhner away from him.

Buhner's final home run came, perhaps appropriately, in Yankee Stadium during the 2001 American League Championship Series. He knew at the time that it might be his last home-run trot.

"I took my time on that one," he said. "I wasn't 100 percent shutting the window because I didn't know how the winter would go."

He'd wanted to come back in 2002, but years of injuries had taken their toll.

"When the doctors come up to you and say they can't give you a passing grade on the physical, when they say you need to seriously think about retiring," he said, "I knew that was the end."

Dan Wilson: The Quiet Pillar of Strength

Lou Piniella was managing the Reds when a young catcher caught his eye at spring training in 1991. Dan Wilson, the Reds' first-round draft pick in 1990, had come into camp and displayed good hands and a solid work ethic.

"We noticed right away he could catch and throw," Piniella said. "He had real good hands behind home plate and he gave a nice target. Our pitchers always wanted to know if Danny was going to catch because they liked throwing to him."

Piniella became the Mariners' manager in 1993 and, by no coincidence, Wilson was on the team a year later. Mariners general manager Woody Woodward traded pitcher Erik Hanson and second baseman Bret Boone to the Reds for relief pitcher Bobby Ayala and Wilson.

Wilson's value to the Mariners won't show in his offensive numbers. He retired after the 2005 season with .262 batting average, 88 home runs, and 519 RBIs in 14 major-league seasons.

Defensively, in the way he caught, threw, and handled a pitching staff, Wilson's value was immeasurable. He committed 42 passed balls and 45 errors in 10,360⅔ innings, finishing his career with a .995 fielding percentage.

He didn't go out with a batting title or championship ring, but Wilson made himself an accomplished catcher because of his preparation, his competitiveness, his toughness, and his ability to put the team ahead of any individual pursuit.

Catcher Dan Wilson dives back to first base.
Photo by Dan Bates/The Herald of Everett, WA

Wilson made the American League All-Star team in 1996 and he batted a career-high .295 in 2000.

"There was always a question of whether Danny would hit," Piniella said. "But I liked him in big-game situations, in RBI situations. He could squeeze, hit-and-run; he stole a few bases. And he was always prepared. Sometimes I had to over-prepare just to make sure I knew what I was talking about when I talked to Danny."

When Wilson retired and was asked to look back on his career, especially his 12 seasons with the Mariners, he didn't focus on the moments of individual glory. It was typical of such a consummate team player.

"Just stepping on the field at Safeco Field is somewhat of an accomplishment, to have this beautiful stadium," he said. "To see how things have changed baseball-wise in Seattle over the last 12 years, it's pretty amazing.

"It was a team effort. That's satisfying."

CHAPTER THIRTEEN

The Rise to a Championship

LEE ELIA KNOWS WHEN THE MARINERS began the transformation from a team always striving for a championship to one that finally won it.

"We came together when the roof caved in," said Elia, the former hitting coach under manager Lou Piniella.

He wasn't speaking in a figurative sense.

The Mariners were taking early batting practice the afternoon of their game against the Baltimore Orioles on July 19, 1994, when Elia, leaning against the batting cage, heard a loud "ka-boom!"

"I looked back and saw a little dust, and I just thought somebody dropped something," he said. "We went back to hitting, and then two or three minutes later, 'ka-boom!' again. Next thing we know, people are pulling us off the field."

The Mariners never stepped into the Kingdome again that year.

Four ceiling tiles weighing 26 pounds each came loose from the underside of the dome's concrete roof and crashed into the seats behind home plate. The Kingdome was closed for four months as the remainder of the 40,000 tiles were removed and the underside of the roof resurfaced.

The Mariners, meanwhile, were ousted from their home park for the rest of the season and forced into the longest road trip in team history. They played 20 games over the next 22 days, traveling a record 10,425 miles. Through it all, the Mariners came together as a team, Elia said.

"If you liked a guy or hated him, it didn't matter, you were with him," he said. "If there were any anxieties between one guy and another, they got cleaned out. It was like being on an island. You had nowhere else to go, and I think the guys bonded."

They bonded and they won.

The Mariners, last in the American League West and seven games behind the first-place Texas Rangers when they began their long trip, won nine of 10 games during one stretch, including six straight victories. They had climbed within two games of first place in the standings and were riding a wave of momentum to the top.

Then the baseball world stood still.

Major-league players went on strike August 12, wiping out the end of the 1994 season, the World Series, and the Mariners' impressive run of success. They thought they could have won the AL West had the season continued. Now all they could hope was that the momentum they rode when the season ended would continue when, or if, the 1995 season began.

"That winter, Lou and I talked about how great it would be if it carried over the following year," Elia said. "Look at the people we had. We had Junior and Jay and Edgar, we had Randy Johnson, Chris Bosio, and Norm Charlton. We had Tino Martinez and Mike Blowers. What a bunch."

Because of the strike, however, nobody knew when those guys would get together again. When spring training began, teams opened their clubhouses to replacement players and the exhibition season began with some rag-tag baseball that was hardly major-league quality.

A federal injunction against the owners ended the strike on April 2 and, after an abbreviated spring training for the regulars that lasted through much of the month, the season began April 25.

The Mariners won six of their first seven games, quickly establishing themselves as a competitive team. It seemed clear from the beginning that their lineup, from top to bottom, would score plenty of runs.

The key, of course, was the man in the middle, Ken Griffey Jr.

The Worst Break

The Mariners were on their way to an 8-3 victory over the Orioles on May 26 when the season arrived at a make-or-break moment.

Kevin Bass launched a fly to deep right-center field, but Ken Griffey Jr. had it tracked from the moment it left the bat. Griffey arrived at the wall just as the ball did and, with a "Spider-Man" leap high on the padding, he made a backhand grab.

Griffey also crashed hard into the wall, and his glove twisted awkwardly on impact. Alex Diaz, playing right field because Jay Buhner was injured, immediately went to Griffey's side and signaled for help from the dugout.

On the bench, Buhner kept saying to himself, "Get up, Junior. Get up."

"We would see Junior run into something hard all the time, but he would get up and shake it off," Buhner said. "He was like Wile E. Coyote, always getting crushed and shaking it off and going right back at it. We'd always seen Junior take a beating and bounce right back."

Griffey wasn't bouncing back from this. Trainer Rick Griffin sprinted from the dugout and met Griffey as he walked in from the outfield.

"I broke my wrist," Griffey told him.

"How do you know?" Griffin said.

"Just look at it," Griffey said.

Griffin did, and what he saw were grossly twisted bones between Griffey's right forearm and hand. He'd shattered both bones in the wrist.

"How long am I going to be out?" Griffey asked as he walked off the field.

Doctors said 10 weeks at least, and they surgically inserted a plate and several screws into the wrist to stabilize it.

Griffey missed 73 games and the Mariners did their best to stay in contention without him. When Griffey returned on August 15, the Mariners were 51-49 and 11½ games behind the California Angels, who were running away with the American League West Division. The Angels were 10½ ahead of second-place Texas.

Still, the Mariners felt good that they hadn't fallen apart after Griffey's injury.

"One of two things could have happened when Junior was hurt," third baseman Mike Blowers said. "We could have folded the tents. But there also was an opportunity for a lot of people, myself included, to do some things. It was a time to become more aggressive and find out about ourselves. I don't think it was a coincidence that it had a big impact on a number of us having our career years."

Blowers hit 23 home runs and drove in 96 runs that year, by far the best of his 11-year career. First baseman Tino Martinez had 31 homers and 111 RBIs in a season that launched his stellar career. Buhner had the first of his three straight seasons with at least 40 home runs and 100 RBIs. DH Edgar Martinez won the American League batting title with a .356 average, and he led the league with 52 doubles and 121 runs.

More than those front-line players, the Mariners of 1995 were a team of unsung heroes.

Rich Amaral and Alex Diaz platooned in center field while Griffey was out, and they contributed both offensively and defensively. Amaral, who'd spent nine years in the minors before he broke in with the Mariners in 1991, batted .282. Diaz made diving catches in center and contributed offensively. His two-run homer in the sixth inning on June 27 pulled the Mariners past the A's in a 6-4 victory.

Doug Strange hit a game-tying, ninth-inning home run on September 19, and the Mariners went on to beat the Rangers.

The Mariners also made roster moves that bolstered the team.

General manager Woody Woodward, blessed with ownership's approval to raise the player payroll, obtained pitcher Andy Benes from the Padres at the July 31 trade deadline. Benes went 7-2 in 12 starts the rest of the season.

On August 15, the day Griffey returned to the lineup, the Mariners got speedy Vince Coleman in a trade with the Royals. Coleman, near the end of his career, became the leadoff hitter, batted .290 and stole 16 bases in the final 40 games.

Griffey, meanwhile, had endured a summer of grueling rehab to get back in the lineup.

"Junior would come in every day that he was hurt and tell the guys, 'Just keep it close. I'll take you there in September,'" Elia said. "Some of us coaches started taking him down in the hitting tunnel where nobody ever saw us, and we would pound him hard, make his hands work. And when he came back, he was ready."

Griffey got a hit in each of his first four games after he returned but hadn't hit a home run. Then, in a Sunday afternoon game against the Red Sox at the Kingdome, he went 3-for-4 and homered off Rheal Cormier, only his eighth home run of the season. The Mariners lost 7-6 in that one to drop 12½ games behind the first-place Angels, but they felt good knowing that Griffey's home-run stroke had returned. He homered again the next night in a 6-0 victory over the Orioles.

The Yankees arrived for a four-game series beginning Thursday, August 24, and the Griffey of old returned when the Mariners needed him most. The Yankees scored six runs in the fourth inning and led the Mariners 7-6 going into the bottom of the ninth inning with closer John Wetteland on the mound.

Wetteland got two quick outs but walked Coleman, who then stole both second and third with Joey Cora batting. Cora singled to left, scoring Coleman with the tying run and bringing Griffey to the plate. Wetteland tried to jam Griffey, but he jumped on that pitch and drove it into the upper deck in right field to give the Mariners a 9-7 victory.

The Mariners considered that victory as the launching point of their amazing late-season surge to the division title.

"My biggest concern when Junior came back was how he would be able to hit after such a nasty injury to his wrist," Blowers said. "That pitch was up and in on Junior, and he was able to get on top of it and hit it out of the ballpark. When he did that, we all knew we had something. We knew that the best player in the game was back."

It was the first game-ending home run of Griffey's career.

"Junior learned something about himself in that game," Buhner said. "It was a moment when he realized, 'I've got it back.' Mentally, that's the biggest challenge you face when you come back from an injury like that. You're asking yourself, 'Am I really ready?'"

He was, and the Mariners rode that home run into a late-season surge that made them champions.

A September to Remember

The Mariners won three of four games from the Yankees in that late-August series. Then they pounded the Red Sox 11-2 on August 31 and began the final month of the season with five victories in seven games.

The first-place Angels, meanwhile, were struggling.

They lost six straight to finish August, and their lead in the AL West was seven and a half games over the Mariners and Rangers, who were tied for second. September was no kinder to the Angels, who lost six of their next seven games. When the Mariners returned home September 8 to begin a three-game series against the Royals, they were six games out and needing the finish of all finishes if they hoped to remain in contention for the division title.

There was more than one carrot to chase, however.

Baseball had gone to an extra round of playoffs for the 1995 season, with one team from each league qualifying as the wild-card entry into the postseason. That became important when the Mariners swept all three games from the Royals but gained only a game in the standings because the Angels took two of three from Minnesota.

Still six and a half games behind the Angels, the sweep of the Royals pushed the Mariners past the Yankees in the wild-card standings by a half-game, and an early case of playoff fever was starting to spread in Seattle. Newspapers began printing the wild-card standings on their sports covers, and the Mariners themselves got into it by hanging a "Wild Card" banner high in the Kingdome.

Jay Buhner, coming out for early batting practice one afternoon, noticed the banner and became livid.

"Who put that up?" he screamed at workers who were preparing the stadium for that night's game. "Somebody get up there and take that f---ing thing down! If anybody has a problem with it, come talk to me!"

Then he told his teammates, "We're going to win the West. We're not going to settle for the wild card."

The Mariners beat the Twins two out of three but couldn't gain ground on the Angels, who also won two of three from the White Sox.

Randy Johnson. *Photo courtesy of the Seattle Mariners*

With 16 games to play, the Mariners were five and a half games out of first place. The odds remained steep, but they knew the Angels would feel the pressure if they kept winning. Buhner hit a three-run homer in the eighth inning and the Mariners beat the Twins 7-4 on September 13, and the comeback nature of Mariners' victories had created confidence in the clubhouse.

Soon, what once seemed impossible became reality.

The Mariners won eight of the next nine games, taking two of three from the White Sox and sweeping both the Rangers and A's, while the Angels lost eight straight to the Royals, A's, and Rangers.

As exciting as the race had become, the fans in Seattle weren't exactly climbing over each other to get into the Kingdome. Crowds for their early September home series were larger than the 5,000 that usually showed up that time of the year, but still small considering the circumstances—between 12,000 and 18,000.

Besides the division race, the Mariners drew extra scrutiny in September of 1995, not all of it positive.

The owners had lobbied hard to replace the Kingdome with a new retractable-roof outdoor stadium, and their threat was clear: If a new stadium wasn't built, the team would be put up for sale and, likely, moved out of Seattle, probably to St. Petersburg, Florida.

The issue spawned a healthy debate between those who believed Major League Baseball improved the quality of life in the city and others who argued that spending hundreds of millions of taxpayer dollars on a sports stadium made no sense in the face of other social needs.

The stadium issue would be decided by King County voters on Tuesday, September 19, with a ballot measure that would determine a proposed sales tax increase from 8.2 percent to 8.3 percent.

When the Mariners returned for their final homestand on September 18, Ken Griffey Jr. issued a plea for fans to step up their support the team—at the turnstiles if not at the polls.

"We're not asking for 60,000, but 25,000 or 30,000, that would be great," he told reporters. "The last couple of games in the dome you could have put everybody on one level and still had room. You hate to see that.

"Fans have got to forget the owners, forget the players, and remember they've got a major-league team in town. This week they'll decide if they want to keep this team or not. But whether we stay or go, this is the most important part of baseball history in Seattle. I hope they want to be a part of it."

The Mariners beat the Rangers 8-1 in the opener of a three-game series and, combined with the Angels' loss to Oakland, pulled within two games of the AL West lead. The fans had responded to Griffey, with an enthusiastic crowd of 29,515 that turned the Kingdome into a noise chamber.

Earlier in the day, the Mariners recorded another victory. They won a coin flip to determine the home team for a possible one-game playoff should the division finish in a first-place tie at the end of the regular season. They had no idea how important that would be to them less than three weeks later.

Tuesday, September 19—election day—became almost surreal in how the events on the field and at the polls played out. With some fans paying as much attention to the election results on their radios as they were to Dave Niehaus' play-by-play of the game, the Mariners trailed the Rangers 4-2 going to the bottom of the ninth inning.

Adding to the fans' disgust, early election results had the stadium measure failing.

Then manager Lou Piniella sent Doug Strange to the plate as a pinch hitter in the ninth inning, and he clubbed a two-run homer, just his second of the season, to tie the score. Two innings later, Griffey singled to score Strange with the winning run in a 5-4 Mariners victory.

The Mariners left the field trailing the fluttering Angels by one game in the division, then turned on the clubhouse TV to watch the election results. Like the comeback victory in the Kingdome, the stadium measure had turned around, too, with yes votes overtaking the no votes. When the Mariners went to bed that night, they were on the verge of first place in the division and getting their new stadium. Life couldn't have been better for a baseball fan in Seattle.

Newspapers the next morning didn't exactly proclaim victory on the stadium measure, but the results were encouraging. It led by 4,000 votes, but supporters were nervous because 47,000 absentee ballots remained uncounted.

On September 20, the Mariners put postseason tickets on sale in the morning, then continued their roll that night. They beat the Rangers again, 11-3, and achieved a place never seen in franchise history. With the Angels losing again, the M's pulled into a first-place tie in the AL West.

After an off day, the Mariners began a three-game series against the A's on September 22 and 51,500 in the Kingdome witnessed the most dramatic night in franchise history. The A's hushed the crowd by taking an early 6-0 lead, but the Mariners stormed back with six runs in the fourth inning, highlighted by Vince Coleman's grand slam. The A's went back ahead 7-6 and carried that lead to the bottom of the eighth inning, when two more heroes emerged for the Mariners.

Edgar Martinez homered to lead off the eighth, tying the score 7-7, and the Mariners put two runners on base when Rich Amaral singled and Mike Blowers walked. Piniella sent switch-hitting Alex Diaz to pinch hit for Luis Sojo, and the A's brought in left-hander Rick Honeycutt to face him.

Diaz connected for a three-run homer, just his third of the season, stirring the crowd into bedlam and leading to a 10-7 victory. The Angels fell again, their eighth straight loss, and the Mariners took a one-game lead in the division.

Those come-from-behind victories gave birth to a slogan that appeared in newspaper headlines and on home-made signs that fans brought to the Kingdome: Refuse to Lose.

"The more the Angels found weird ways to lose, we were finding unbelievable ways of winning," Buhner said. "Once we got to mid-September, we knew we were going to catch them. We just hoped we wouldn't run out of games."

On September 23, Randy Johnson struck out 15 and pushed his record to 16-2 in a 7-0 shutout of the A's—the Mariners' 10th victory in 11 games—and the Angels lost again to give Seattle a two-game lead in the division.

The next night, Tino Martinez continued the hero-a-day parade when he hit a two-run homer in the bottom of the ninth inning to give the Mariners a 9-8 victory.

The Angels came to Seattle for two games and, after the Mariners beat them 10-2 in the series opener on September 26,

California beat the M's 2-0 on a shutout by Chuck Finley. The Mariners led the Angels by two games with four remaining in the season.

With a magic number of two, all the Mariners needed to clinch a tie for the division title was to win twice in their final four-game series at Texas. They did that in the first two games, beating the Rangers 6-2 and 4-3.

Things weren't going so well on the stadium vote, which headed toward defeat as absentee ballots were counted. A tally of the ballots on September 25 left the stadium issue trailing by 1,535 votes with only 3,000 ballots left to count.

With serious fears that Seattle could lose its team, government leaders called a special meeting of state, county, and city officials with Gov. Mike Lowry in Olympia, the state capitol. After a two-and-a-half-hour meeting, they reached an agreement to fund a new stadium, despite what had become a "no" vote on the issue.

"It's in the interest of the quality of life in our state to build a stadium and save the Mariners," Lowry said.

The quality-of-life argument had become easier to sell because of the Mariners' September success.

"Who's to know if we don't put that season together like we did, that we would even be talking about the Seattle Mariners years later," said John McLaren, a coach on Piniella's staff. "It might have been the St. Pete Mariners."

So, having been deemed a state resource as precious as the mountains, trees, and ocean, the Mariners seemed safer in Seattle than they had in years. Now, if only they could finish their weekend mission and clinch the AL West.

The Angels made that difficult. They clubbed Oakland 4-1 and 9-6 in the first two games of their final series, keeping alive their hope of forcing a one-game playoff. The Angels' only chance was to finish a sweep in their final two games against the A's and hope the Mariners faltered in their last two at Texas. That's exactly what happened. The Mariners fell miserably, 9-2 and 9-3 to the Rangers, while the Angels pummeled the A's again, 9-3 and 8-2.

The teams flew to Seattle late Sunday for a Monday afternoon tiebreaker game in the Kingdome, with the winner moving into the first round of the playoffs against the Yankees, who had clinched the American League's wild-card berth.

Despite their tailspin in Texas, the Mariners returned for the tiebreaker feeling confident. They had two huge advantages. By winning the coin flip on September 18, they would play the game in the Kingdome, where the volume of more than 52,000 fans had become a factor in their September surge. And with Randy Johnson starting, even on just three days of rest, it wouldn't take many runs for the Mariners to win.

"When we got on that plane in Texas, there was no doubt in anybody's mind that we were going to win that game," third baseman Mike Blowers said. "We knew what we were going to get out of Randy. We felt if we could score three runs, we would win that game."

The Angels entered the game just as confident, having reversed their late-season plummet with the four-game sweep of the A's.

"Once we tied it, we went to Seattle confident, and it didn't matter who we were going to face," said Eduardo Perez, a young infielder with the Angels. "We knew they were going to throw the Unit, we just didn't know what our lineup would be. We figured it would be like we'd done before during the season, when we had all righties when we faced him."

Instead, California manager Marcel Lachemann's lineup included two left-handed hitters, Jim Edmonds and Garret Anderson, perhaps because of what the Angels had done to Johnson the last time they met him. With Edmonds and Anderson facing the Mariners' ace for the first time, the Angels pounded Johnson in a 7-2 victory on August 1.

"It was a crazy situation," Perez, said. "But we thought we couldn't lose."

The Angels started left-hander Mark Langston, the former Mariner who had been one of the organization's best players in the 1980s before they traded him away. Langston, a 15-game winner, matched Johnson inning-for-inning early in the game, then blinked.

The Mariners broke a scoreless tie in the fifth against Langston with a walk and two hits, scoring the first run of the game on Vince Coleman's RBI single. Johnson didn't allow a baserunner through 5⅔ innings before Rex Hudler singled.

In the seventh, the Mariners gave Johnson all the runs he needed on one of the most famous plays in franchise history.

They loaded the bases with one out against Langston, who got another out before facing Luis Sojo. The veteran infielder from Venezuela hit a broken-bat cue shot down the right-field line, past first baseman J.T. Snow and into the Angels' bullpen, where relief pitchers scattered and right fielder Tim Salmon had to dig the ball from under the bench.

All three Mariners scored and, when Langston's relay throw flew past catcher Andy Allanson, Sojo sprinted home from third base. It became known as the "Everybody Scores" play, based on the radio call by Mariners announcer Rick Rizzs, and the Mariners led 5-0.

"Once it got away from us, Randy was determined," the Angels' Perez said. "That's what took them to the next level. He was as dominating as he could be."

The Mariners scored four more runs in the eighth to take a 9-0 lead and Johnson, after allowing Tony Phillips' leadoff homer in the ninth, breezed through the Angels the rest of the way. He struck out Salmon on a called third strike for the final out, setting off a wild celebration both on the field and in the stands at the Kingdome.

"You couldn't hear anything," Blowers said. "It was not only loud, but it felt extremely hot down on the field. It was as warm as I've ever been in that place."

The Mariners partied hard after that game, spraying champagne in the clubhouse and reveling in their first championship. The celebration was brief, however, because they had to be on the field at Yankee Stadium in less than 24 hours, and their plane was already warming up.

Comeback Against the Yankees

During the Mariners' flight to New York, you wouldn't have known if they'd won or lost just hours earlier.

"I don't think I've ever been more tired in my life," third baseman Mike Blowers said. "It was more the emotional part of it all. That's one of the few times I've actually slept on a flight."

The Mariners had every reason to walk into Yankee Stadium both physically and emotionally worn out. In less than two days, they'd flown from Texas to Seattle, won the biggest game of their lives, then high-tailed it from Seattle to New York for Game 1 of the American League Division Series.

"It was tough," bench coach Lee Elia said. "But you get to a point in postseason play where you don't allow yourself to think of that stuff."

Adrenaline and Ken Griffey Jr. nearly carried the Mariners to victory in the series opener. Griffey homered twice, his seventh-inning blow tying the score 4-4, but the Mariners' bullpen ran dry, allowing four runs in the seventh and one in the eighth as the Yankees won 9-6.

The Mariners scored twice in the seventh inning of Game 2 to take a 4-3 lead, but Paul O'Neill's home run in the bottom of the seventh tied the score 4-4. Griffey homered to give the Mariners a 5-4 lead in the 12th, but Ruben Sierra's RBI double scored Jorge Posada to tie the game again.

Three innings later in a driving rain, Yankees catcher Jim Leyritz ended a five-hour, 12-minute epic when he drove a pitch from Tim Belcher for a two-run homer. The 7-5 victory put the Yankees in a commanding position in the best-of-five series, leaving them just one victory from clinching the series, which headed back to Seattle for Game 3 and, if needed, Games 4 and 5.

On the flight back home, Blowers and first baseman Tino Martinez discussed how the team had fallen to the brink of elimination, and how they hoped to reward the fans in Seattle—and themselves—with at least one postseason victory.

"We'd come way too far for this to happen," Blowers said. "We had to win at least one playoff game because, as a player, you never know if you're ever going to get back."

Randy Johnson outpitched Jack McDowell and the Mariners won 7-4 in Game 3. The Mariners knew they'd cleared a big hurdle to win a game over the Yankees—"It was a sense of relief," Blowers said—but it also renewed their hunger to win the series.

"You know what?" Jay Buhner asked Blowers. "If we win again tomorrow night, all the pressure is on them for Game 5."

The next night, the Yankees played like there was no pressure at all. They blistered Mariners starter Chris Bosio early, scoring five runs in the first three innings. The 57,180 in the Kingdome, so raucous during the Mariners' September stretch drive, had fallen silent.

Then Edgar Martinez changed the series. He clubbed a three-run homer in the third inning, and the Mariners scored four times to pull within a run at 5-4.

The Mariners scored an unearned run in the fifth inning to tie the score, and Ken Griffey Jr. homered in the sixth for a 6-5 lead. The Yankees tied it again in the top of the eighth when Norm Charlton threw a wild pitch, but the Mariners threatened again in the bottom of the eighth against John Wetteland.

Vince Coleman walked, Joey Cora reached on a bunt single, and Wetteland hit Griffey with a pitch to load the bases. That brought Martinez to the plate, and he crushed a two-ball, two-strike pitch from Wetteland over the center-field fence for a grand slam and a 10-6 Mariners lead. His seven RBIs in the game set a major-league postseason record.

Jay Buhner followed with a solo homer off reliever Steve Howe for an 11-6 score, and the Yankees put together a mild rally against Charlton and Bobby Ayala in the ninth, scoring twice, before Bill Risley got the final two outs.

The victory sent the Mariners into what amounted to another one-game playoff in the deciding Game 5 at the Kingdome. They'd have to win it this time without their ace, Randy Johnson, who was unavailable to start because he'd pitched two days earlier.

Andy Benes got the ball and he held the Yankees to four hits and four runs in 6⅔ innings. David Cone had held the Mariners to seven hits and single runs in the third and fourth innings, and the Yankees led 4-2 going into the bottom of the eighth.

Griffey hit a one-out homer to make it 4-3 before Cone, who was running out of gas, walked Tino Martinez, gave up a single to Buhner and walked Alex Diaz to load the bases. Piniella sent his super sub, Doug Strange, to pinch hit for catcher Dan Wilson, and Cone walked Strange to force in a run, tying the score 4-4.

Yankees manager Buck Showalter replaced Cone with Mariano Rivera, a rookie right-hander who'd started 10 games for the Yankees that year. Rivera, showing a wicked fastball that would make him one of baseball's greatest closers in future years, finished off the Mariners in the eighth.

Meanwhile, Randy Johnson, who'd started two days earlier, began warming up in the Mariners' bullpen. After the first two Yankees in the ninth reached base, Piniella brought Johnson into the game, and he got three straight outs to leave the score tied 4-4.

Vince Coleman led off the ninth with a single and reached second on Joey Cora's sacrifice bunt. Rivera intentionally walked Griffey before Showalter went to his bullpen again, bringing in Jack McDowell, the Yankees' starter in Game 3. The strategy worked, and McDowell got out of the ninth.

The two starters-turned-relievers, Johnson and McDowell, made it through the 10th inning before the Yankees got to Johnson in the 11th. He walked leadoff hitter Mike Stanley, who was replaced by pinch runner Pat Kelly. Kelly reached second on Tony Fernandez's sacrifice bunt, then scored when Randy Velarde singled, giving the Yankees a 5-4 lead. Johnson struck out Jim Leyritz and Paul O'Neill to get out of the inning, and the Mariners came to bat in the bottom of the 11th needing a run to avoid elimination.

Joey Cora started it by dropping a perfect drag bunt, barely eluding first baseman Don Mattingly's tag to reach with a leadoff single. That brought up Griffey, and nearly everyone in the Kingdome got to their feet and pointed to the right-field seats, where he'd hit so many home runs in his career. Griffey couldn't end the game, but he kept it going with a single to center, sending Cora to third representing the tying run with nobody out.

With Edgar Martinez coming to bat, the Mariners couldn't have asked for a better situation. Martinez had thrashed the Yankees' pitching all series, going 11-for-20 up to that at-bat. McDowell had been careful with Martinez in Game 3, getting him to ground out in his first at-bat, then walking him his next two times up.

This time, McDowell tried to sneak a slider past Martinez and he left it up and over the plate. Martinez turned on it, driving the ball into the left-field corner. Cora scored easily and Griffey steamed around second, gaining speed with his long, powerful stride.

Third-base coach Sam Perlozzo waved Griffey home, boldly defying baseball logic. By playing it safe and stopping Griffey there, the Mariners still would have a runner on third with nobody out, with Jay Buhner, Mike Blowers, and Tino Martinez coming up.

There was no stop sign.

"Sammy made the gamble of all gambles by sending Junior," Elia said. "It's going to be a bang-bang play at the plate, and if he's out, you never know what might happen."

Griffey's stride got longer and stronger, and he charged around third like a thoroughbred headed for the wire. He slid into the plate well ahead of the throw, winning the game and the series, sending the Kingdome into a frenzy and the Mariners into the American League Championship Series against the Cleveland Indians.

Mariners vs. Indians: One Step From the World Series

The euphoria of the Mariners' victory over the Yankees lasted as long as it took anyone to realize their pitching was a mess for the ALCS. Randy Johnson wouldn't be available until Game 3 in Cleveland, and the Mariners settled on 22-year-old rookie right-hander Bob Wolcott, who wasn't even on the roster for the series against the Yankees, to face the powerful Indians in Game 1.

Wolcott started that game like an unsteady rookie.

He walked the first three hitters—Kenny Lofton, Omar Vizquel, and Carlos Baerga—then faced a pitcher's nightmare, slugger Albert Belle with the bases loaded and nobody out. Before Belle came to the plate, Mariners manager Lou Piniella took one of his slow, meandering walks to the mound.

Third baseman Mike Blowers, who would normally stick an ear into such a conversation, stayed away.

"I didn't go there because I didn't know what Lou was going to do," Blowers said. "I didn't know if he would undress Bobby or pat him on the back."

Piniella, known to have melted struggling young pitchers with his blistering sermons on the mound, delivered a gentle message to Wolcott.

"Son, we don't have anybody else," Piniella said. "You're going to be out here if we give up 20 runs, 10 runs, or zero runs. You could be home in Oregon by now fishing, so just settle down, and let's get these guys out."

In just his seventh major-league start, Wolcott did just as he was told. He struck out Belle and got Eddie Murray on a foul popup, then was saved by his defense. Jim Thome hit a hard one-hopper up the middle, but second baseman Joey Cora made a diving stop and, from his knees, threw Thome out at first base for the third out.

Indians manager Mike Hargrove, who would become the Mariners' manager in 2005, was asked if he had that situation 100 times—bases loaded, nobody out and the beef of that batting order coming up—how often the Indians would be held without a run.

"Once," Hargrove said. "That one."

Blowers hit a two-run homer, Luis Sojo hit an RBI double, and Wolcott held the Indians to eight hits and two runs in seven innings as the Mariners won the series opener 3-2.

Orel Hershiser held the Mariners to four hits in eight innings, leading the Indians to a 5-2 victory in Game 2, sending the series back to Cleveland for Games 3, 4 and 5.

Johnson, rested from his draining weekend against the Yankees, limited the Indians to one run entering the eighth inning. The Mariners led 2-1 in the eighth when right fielder Jay Buhner misplayed Alvaro Espinoza's fly, leading to an unearned run that tied the score.

The game progressed into the 11th when the Mariners put two runners on base and Buhner batted against right-hander Eric Plunk. Three innings after his defensive gaffe let the Indians back into the game, Buhner decided it with a three-run homer that gave the Mariners a 5-2 victory and a 2-1 lead in the series.

The Indians pummeled the Mariners 7-0 the next night, and the M's faced the difficult chore of trying to beat Hershiser in the critical Game 5. Hershiser was tough again, holding the Mariners to two runs in six innings, and Mariners starter Chris Bosio kept the game close by limiting the Indians to three runs.

The Indians led 3-2 when Vince Coleman gave the Mariners an opportunity to tie the score in the eighth, walking with one out and stealing second against Plunk. That set up a sequence of subtle events, unknown to most fans, that may have determined not only who won the game, but also the series, Mariners hitting coach Lee Elia said.

"We've got Coleman on second base, and we're trying to get him to steal because their guy is slow to the plate," Elia said.

Indians shortstop Omar Vizquel, the former Mariner, saw Coleman's growing lead off the bag and sensed that something was up, Elia said.

"On the first pitch, nobody smelled a thing," Elia said. "But on the second pitch, Omar realized this guy had too much of a lead and he shortened up about three steps."

Coleman didn't run on the third pitch, either.

"So now Omar really slides over, about five or six yards from his original spot," Elia said.

Sojo lashed at the fourth pitch and smoked a line drive right at Vizquel, who had positioned himself perfectly to catch the ball and trap Coleman off the bag for a double play that ended the threat.

"If Luis hits that ball a pitch or two earlier, Omar wouldn't have been there and that ball might have gone to the wall," Elia said.

If it had gone to the wall, the Mariners would have tied the score and put another runner on base in scoring position.

"Was it game-changing? It probably was," Hargrove said. "If they score that run, it's a different scenario. We won that game by one run."

Back in Seattle for Game 6 with a 3-2 series lead, the Indians still didn't feel at ease. They had their ace, Dennis Martinez, on the mound for that one, but the Mariners were bringing back Randy Johnson on three days of rest.

Hargrove knew that anything could happen in a game played at the Kingdome.

"The Mariners doing what they had done all year didn't make you feel all that good," Hargrove said. "The Mariners had a real good team and it seemed like destiny was on their side. I swore if I ever saw another Refuse to Lose sign I was going to just die. Everywhere you looked there was a Refuse to Lose sign in everybody's window, on the office buildings and every storefront. After a while, you get to thinking that maybe there's something to that."

Martinez was brilliant for the Indians in Game 6, pitching seven shutout innings, and Johnson held on as long as he could, clearly not as sharp as he'd been throughout the postseason.

"We rode his back for half that season," Blowers said. "But it looked to me like from the start Randy was out of gas. He was going up against the best lineup in the league, and you could tell he was just off."

The Indians took a 1-0 lead in the fifth on Kenny Lofton's RBI single, and they made it 4-0 with three runs in the eighth. Two of those scored on a passed ball by Wilson, including the speedy Lofton from second base.

"When Lofton scored from second base on that one play, it seemed like the air went right out of the building," Hargrove said. "The way we added on was just a real nail in the coffin."

Piniella pulled Johnson, who for the first time in months couldn't save the Mariners. They never got another baserunner and the Indians finished off a 4-0 victory that sent them to the World Series.

After the final out, the Mariners lingered in their dugout—Joey Cora sat on the bench sobbing in the arms of rookie shortstop Alex Rodriguez—before quietly heading back to their clubhouse.

Then something marvelous happened.

All but a few among the crowd of 58,489 remained in the building. The Mariners' fans had established a true love for that team, and they were reluctant to walk away a final time. They politely saluted the celebrating Indians, then began one last cheer for the Mariners with an ovation that grew louder and louder.

Underneath the grandstands, Piniella addressed the Mariners, thanking them for the effort that resulted in such a memorable season.

"Then somebody came in and said something quietly to Lou," Blowers said. "He told us to get our pants and shirts back on, that the crowd was still back out there and we needed to go out and show our appreciation."

When the Mariners reached the field again, 15 minutes after the final out, the Kingdome remained packed.

"We were all shocked at the amount of people who were there and how loud the ovation was when we came back out," Blowers said. "I'd never seen anything like it before."

Months and years later, those who were part of the Mariners' magnificent ride remember it as one of the best times in their careers. Many of them could only wonder what that team might have accomplished if just a few more breaks had gone their way.

What if Omar Vizquel hadn't turned that game-changing double play for the Indians in Game 5?

What if the one-game playoff against the Angels hadn't wrinkled the Mariners' pitching rotation?

What if Randy Johnson had been able to pitch throughout the postseason with regular rest? Could he have been a different pitcher in Game 6 against the Indians and given the Mariners a Game 7 opportunity to reach the World Series?

"When you think about the Mariners of '95, the only shame is that we didn't go to the World Series," Elia said. "If we hadn't had that one-game playoff against the Angels, when we had to use the Unit, I still feel in my heart that the whole thing would have turned out different."

CHAPTER FOURTEEN

Building a Winner Without Johnson, Junior, A-Rod

THE MARINERS TRIED TO RECAPTURE THE MAGIC OF 1995 but never came close through the remainder of the 1990s.

They were a good team, no doubt, and after the front office made such additions as first baseman Paul Sorrento and pitchers Jamie Moyer and Jeff Fassero, the Mariners won the AL West again in 1997. The Baltimore Orioles smothered them with pitching in the first round of the playoffs, winning three of four to eliminate the Mariners.

The Mariners, however, were a changing team as the decade went on.

In 1998, they dealt unhappy pitcher Randy Johnson to the Houston Astros at the trade deadline. Before the 2000 season, center fielder Ken Griffey Jr. was gone, traded to the Cincinnati Reds. And a year later, shortstop Alex Rodriguez shunned the Mariners' five-year, $95 million offer and jumped at a deal he couldn't pass up, 10 years and $252 million from the Texas Rangers.

Despite losing their three best players in less than four years, the Mariners remained competitive and returned to the postseason.

Without Johnson in 1999, the Mariners built their rotation around the young pitcher they got from the Astros in return, right-hander Freddy Garcia.

Without Griffey in 2000, they plugged the defensive void in center field with Mike Cameron, one of four players obtained from the Reds in that trade. Then they added smooth-swinging John Olerud at first base, Japanese pitcher Kazuhiro Sasaki at closer and won the American League wild card.

Without Rodriguez in 2001, the Mariners signed Japanese right fielder Ichiro Suzuki, second baseman Bret Boone, and retooled the team to fit the pitching/defense/small-ball style that was needed to win at Safeco Field. They put together the greatest season in American League history and tied baseball's all-time record with 116 regular-season victories.

The Mariners still had Edgar Martinez, Jay Buhner, and Dan Wilson, but they never achieved what they truly wanted, an appearance in the World Series.

"You always wonder what we could have done if we'd been able to put all those components together," said John McLaren, manager Lou Piniella's bench coach on those 2000 and 2001 playoff teams. "What if we could have kept Randy and Junior and Alex, and put them together with Edgar and Cameron and Boone and Ichiro? I understand the financial restraints of the game and I know there's a time when guys move on, but you wonder just what we could have accomplished with all those guys together."

Mike Cameron: Fan Favorite After Griffey

Watching the trade rumors from his home in Georgia, Mike Cameron was no different than any other baseball fan during the off-season between the 1999 and 2000 seasons. The Ken Griffey Jr. saga enthralled him.

It seemed certain that the Mariners would trade Griffey, and it was no secret that he would wind up in Cincinnati. Cameron, the Reds' promising young center fielder, knew such a trade would dramatically change his role, if not the team he played for as well.

Trade rumors ran wild, but the name Cameron rarely heard was his own.

"The only person I heard being mentioned was Pokey," Cameron said.

Pokey Reese was the name that appeared in the Seattle newspapers more than any other. And rightfully so. The Mariners needed a second baseman, and Reese not only played the position well, he could provide the type of offense the M's needed, having hit .285 and stolen 38 bases in 1999. Reese could provide the type of athleticism that manager Lou Piniella was seeking.

"All I heard was Pokey, Pokey Pokey," Cameron said. "But all of a sudden, the trade was made and there were four of us going to Seattle."

Mariners general manager Pat Gillick swung a five-player trade—Griffey to the Reds for pitchers Brett Tomko and Jake Meyer, minor-league infielder Antonio Perez and, of course, Cameron.

The trade surprised Cameron, who had played only one season in Cincinnati after beginning his career with the Chicago White Sox.

"I was still trying to get a sense of who I was as a player at the time," he said. "I was highly regarded with the White Sox and I thought that was going to be my team forever, but I had a bad sophomore season and got traded to the Reds. We almost got to the playoffs the last day of the season, and we were so young and had so many good young players on the team that I thought we would stay together forever."

In an era of free agency and frequent player movement, no team stays together long. Cameron not only had to face the difficult fact that he had been traded, but also that he was replacing a Mariners legend.

When the trade was announced, Mariners fans were irate. They scolded Gillick on radio talk shows and roasted him in newspaper letters to the editor. They said the Reds stole the Mariners blind, that Gillick gave away the franchise in exchange for four barely known players.

Cameron understood the fans' lament.

"I knew it would be a difficult task to be comfortable," he said. "There was no way possible that anybody could come in and fill Junior's shoes. He'd been here since he was 19, and he was what people here were accustomed to seeing."

Cameron, however, had extreme confidence in his ability to play center field, and that gave him comfort. So did the team he was coming to. The Mariners were far from a one-man team with Griffey, and without him they still had Alex Rodriguez, Edgar

Martinez, Dan Wilson, and Jay Buhner, plus veteran newcomers John Olerud, Mark McLemore, and Stan Javier.

"I knew I was coming to a good team, and if all I did was just play, the other things would take care of themselves," Cameron said.

Still, there was no mistaking that the spotlight was directed at Cameron. Confident in his ability to play center field, he welcomed it.

"I didn't really worry about it until I got to Seattle," he said. "Everybody got a chance to see me at spring training, and that was an opportunity for me to show what I could do. I worked really hard to get to the level where I felt they wouldn't miss anything without Griffey out there, even though I knew that wasn't possible."

Cameron tip-toed through the first three games, playing well in center field and, after going 0-for-4 in the season opener against the Red Sox, warming up with the bat. In the second game, he went 2-for-5, including a triple, to help the Mariners beat the Red Sox. The following night, in the third game, he hit his first home run as a Mariner in another victory.

The Yankees came to Seattle for the Mariners' first weekend series of 2000, and Safeco Field was filled nearly to capacity on Friday, April 7. In the eighth inning, as the Mariners tried to protect a 6-3 lead, Cameron literally leaped into the welcoming arms of the fans who'd been so uneasy after losing Griffey.

Derek Jeter, who had homered early in the game, launched a high fly off Mariners reliever Paul Abbott, and the ball seemed headed for the patio area beyond the center-field fence. Cameron sprinted to the warning track and leaped high against the wall. When he came down, he had the ball in the webbing of his glove, robbing Jeter of a home run.

"I had a good bead on it," Cameron said. "I snow-coned it in my glove and brought it back over the fence. It felt like it happened in slow motion, where I was able to catch the ball and see it slipping out of my glove, and then pop it back in there."

Better than saving a run against the Yankees, that magnificent leap became the moment Mariners fans accepted Cameron. As he jogged back to the dugout after the third out, the crowd at Safeco Field gave him a long, loud standing ovation.

"I got chills," Cameron said. "It was a special moment for me. That catch allowed the city to feel comfortable with the type of player they had. I'd made those catches all the time in Chicago and Cincinnati. But the fact that I was able to do it here kind of allowed people to feel comfortable with me."

From an unknown replacement for Griffey, Cameron became the perfect man to patrol the vast center field at the Mariners' new outdoor ballpark, Safeco Field. With deep gaps and heavy marine air, there aren't many no-doubt-about-it home runs at Safeco. High fly balls tend to hang for the outfielders to catch, but it takes speed and a no-fear approach to succeed.

Cameron made every kind of catch—with body-slams into the padding, leaps above the wall, and dives to the turf on bloops in the gaps—and his career flourished in Seattle. He won Gold Glove awards in 2001 and 2003 and, despite his tendency to strike out, he served as a force in the middle of the Mariners' batting order during their playoff runs in 2000 and 2001. His 25 home runs and 110 RBIs in 2001 were career highs.

"I was a good player when I got to Seattle," Cameron said. "After I got here, I started to really grasp what kind of player I was. What helped was that we had the type of players to allow me to flourish the way I wanted to."

If the catch of Jeter's ball in 2000 was the moment Cameron became known as a bona fide replacement for Griffey, his offensive performance on May 2, 2002, served notice to the kind of hitter he was. He hit four home runs that night against the White Sox in Comiskey Park, becoming one of 15 in major-league history to do it.

For one night, he'd accomplished something even the great Griffey hadn't.

"I've had an asterisk by my name as the guy traded for Ken Griffey Jr.," Cameron said that night. "Now maybe I'll have another asterisk."

Alex Rodriguez:
From Most Valuable to Most Vilified

The first day he pulled on a Mariners uniform, Alex Rodriguez made an impression, not only with his bat or his glove.

It was the spring of 1994, and Rodriguez, baseball's first overall draft pick in 1993, worked out for a day with the big-league club.

"The one thing that caught my eye was his eagerness to learn," said John McLaren, the Mariners' bullpen coach then. "He asked a lot of questions and he left a nice impression that he really, really enjoyed playing the game of baseball."

Only a few months later, Rodriguez was in the majors. He'd progressed through the Class-A and Double-A levels quickly and manager Lou Piniella called him up just before the All-Star break. At 18, he became baseball's youngest major leaguer since Jose Rijo with the Mets at 18 in 1984.

"You could tell he had a world of talent," McLaren said.

Being so young, Rodriguez struggled. He batted just .204 in 17 games before the Mariners sent him back to the minors in 1994, and the next year, after spending the first month at the Triple-A level, Rodriguez batted .232 with five home runs and 19 RBIs in 48 games with the Mariners.

"He was a baby-faced kid then," McLaren said. "You could see that he was bug-eyed that first year, looking at players like Ken Griffey Jr., who he idolized, and Randy Johnson, Jay Buhner, and Edgar Martinez. Kenny talked with him about handling the pressures of being a star, and all of those guys helped him become the player he is."

Rodriguez experienced an adjustment period, albeit a short one.

Like many young players, he loved to pull the ball, and the Mariners knew he would struggle if he didn't hit to all fields. Piniella and hitting coach Lee Elia worked with Rodriguez, teaching him to stay inside the ball and drive it to right-center field.

The results were almost immediate. In 1996, Rodriguez hit 35 home runs and drove in 123, led the league with a .358 batting average, made the All-Star team and won the Player of the Year award.

Edgar Martinez congratulates Alex Rodriguez at the plate after A-Rod's home run. *Photo by Justin Best/The Herald of Everett, WA*

"He learned how to hit in a hurry," McLaren said. "You knew the natural talent was there, and Lee Elia and Lou Piniella were the ones who shaped this kid."

Rodriguez's numbers fell off in 1997—23 homers, 84 RBIs and a .300 average—but in 1998 he produced the best all-around year of his career. Rodriguez hit 42 home runs, drove in 124 and stole 46 bases, making him the third player in history, at the time, to hit at least 40 home runs and steal 40 bases in the same season. (Jose Canseco did it in 1988 and Barry Bonds in 1996. Alfonso Soriano became the fourth in 2006.)

As much as Rodriguez meant to the Mariners' lineup, fans who looked at the future of the Mariners began to worry. Griffey would be eligible for free agency after the 1999 season and Rodriguez the following year. Offers by the Mariners to both players in 1999 went nowhere, and Griffey was traded to the Reds the next off-season.

Rodriguez's free-agent season was next, in 2000, and despite hitting 41 homers and driving in 132 runs to help return the Mariners to the playoffs, his future became a frequent topic of concern.

Rodriguez said all the right things to ease the fans' fear of his possible departure. He said the most important criteria for his next team would be its ability to win a championship. The Mariners, who'd taken the Yankees to six games in the 2000 ALCS, seemed as close as any team to that.

The Mariners had understood from Rodriguez's agent, Scott Boras, that he didn't want to be tied to an ultra-long contract. They offered him five years at $95 million, and Rodriguez barely sniffed at it.

The New York Mets courted Rodriguez and then backed away, but Texas Rangers owner Tom Hicks made an offer that Rodriguez couldn't shun—$252 million over 10 years. Rodriguez took it, and Mariners fans became livid.

They never forgave Rodriguez for making such a big deal of his desire to sign with a winning team. The Rangers, with a pitching staff that was in shambles, were many years from being competitive.

Many newspapers used the term "Pay-Rod" in their headlines after he signed the deal. *The Everett Herald* ran a "Pay-Rod Meter" on its website, showing Rodriguez's salary total climbing by the second.

Rodriguez never came close to the championship he said he wanted. While the Mariners charged toward a record-tying 116 victories in 2001, the Rangers finished last in the American League West with a 73-69 record, 43 games behind the first-place M's. The Rangers' 5.71 team ERA was the worst in baseball that year.

When Rodriguez returned with the Rangers to Safeco Field, Mariners fans booed him viciously every time he came to bat or fielded a ball. Some fans threw wads of bills that fluttered from the upper deck. Before his first at-bat after returning as a Ranger, Rodriguez stood in the on-deck circle unaware that a fan in the front row was using a fishing pole to dangle a dollar bill over his head.

Mariners fans heckle Alex Rodriguez after he signed with the Texas Rangers.
Photo by Stephanie S. Cordle/The Herald of Everett, WA

"Alex set down some criteria for what he wanted, but when Tom Hicks came with all that money, the criteria crumbled," McLaren said. "I've been an Alex Rodriguez fan and I always will be. It's a shame that so many people look to pick on the guy, but it goes with the territory."

Mariners Y2K: Return to the Postseason, Without Griffey

If the difficult 1999 season proved anything, it's that the Mariners needed to play a different style of baseball at Safeco Field than they played in the Kingdome.

In the dome, they could sneak a couple of runners on base and wait for a three-run homer. At the new ballpark, where the outfield gaps were big and the cool marine air from nearby Puget Sound turned long balls into outs at the warning track, it would take pitching, defense, and a small-ball attack to win.

Manager Lou Piniella had cried for a more athletic lineup, and when the Mariners got together for spring training in 2000, he had it.

Mike Cameron brought speed, decent power, and a solid glove. The Mariners signed first baseman John Olerud, the former batting champion who grew up in nearby Bellevue, Washington, hoping he could take advantage of Safeco Field's vast spaces and spray the ball to all fields. They added veteran Mark McLemore, an infielder/outfielder who gave Piniella both versatility and speed off the bench, and added 18-year veteran Stan Javier, who could handle the bat in any situation and provide leadership in the clubhouse.

Aaron Sele, another home-state player who grew up in Poulsbo, Washington, signed as a free agent and joined a starting rotation that included Freddy Garcia, Jamie Moyer, Paul Abbott, and John Halama.

The Mariners strengthened the bullpen, one of the club's biggest concerns, by signing Kazuhiro Sasaki, Japan's all-time saves leader, who replaced Jose Mesa at closer. They also acquired hard-throwing Arthur Rhodes, a left-handed relief specialist.

After a 79-victory season in 1999 that left them in third place, Piniella was asked midway through spring training if the 2000 Mariners could win more than 85 games.

"Oh please," he said. "Let's not get too carried away."

After all, the Mariners were trying to move on without Ken Griffey Jr.

They didn't come close to winning 85. They won 91.

A 19-8 record in June propelled the Mariners into first place, one-half game ahead of Oakland, and they steadily increased the margin as the summer went on. By August 11, they led by seven games over the A's.

"We played good ball that year," pitching coach Bryan Price said. "But when we would lose a few games, we'd start to think, 'Hey, maybe we're not as good as we thought we were.'"

The Mariners lost more than a few in August and September, and the A's overtook them for the division lead by winning nine of their final 11 games. The late-season fade forced the Mariners to win their final two games just to reach the postseason as the American

Catcher Dan Wilson and closer Kazuhiro Sasaki.
Photo by Justin Best/The Herald of Everett, WA

League wild-card team. They beat the Angels 21-9 and 5-2, sending them to Chicago for a first-round series against the White Sox.

Piniella did some of his finest managing in that series.

In Game 1, the Mariners and White Sox took a 4-4 tie into extra innings before Mike Cameron singled to lead off the 10th inning against Chicago closer Keith Foulke. Alex Rodriguez flied to left for the first out and, with the dangerous Edgar Martinez hitting, Foulke made numerous throws to first base to keep Cameron close.

Suddenly, Piniella called time out and walked onto the field, not to argue with an umpire but to talk with his baserunner.

"I'd never in my life seen a manager do that," Price said. "You see them go out and talk to a pitcher, but never to a baserunner. I didn't even know it was legal to do that. At first I thought Cameron was injured."

Piniella met Cameron near the first-base coaches' box and whispered something into his ear, then walked back to the dugout. Cameron went back to the bag, smiling.

Piniella, famous for knowing opposing personnel as well as his own, had tipped off Cameron on when it would be best to steal.

"He said if the catcher set up outside, it would be a pitch I could run on, so go," Cameron said. "I mean, the guy calls time out and tells me how to steal a base. Unbelievable."

Cameron stole the base, and Martinez followed with a two-run homer off Foulke. John Olerud, the next hitter, also homered to give the Mariners a 7-4 lead, and closer Kazuhiro Sasaki finished off the White Sox in the bottom of the 10th to notch the Game 1 victory.

The next night, Paul Abbott limited the White Sox to two runs in 5⅔ innings and the Mariners' bullpen—Arthur Rhodes, Jose Mesa, and Kazuhiro Sasaki—held Chicago hitless over the final 3⅓ innings for a 5-2 victory.

With a chance to clinch the series at home, the Mariners started Aaron Sele in Game 3, and he stifled the White Sox on three hits and a run in 7⅓ innings. Chicago starter James Baldwin was nearly as effective, holding the Mariners to three hits and a run in six innings.

With the score tied 1-1, Olerud led off the bottom of the ninth with a wicked smash back to the mound, hitting White Sox reliever Kelly Wunsch in the stomach. Olerud reached second when Wunsch, injured, threw the ball away at first base.

Foulke replaced Wunsch on the mound, and Piniella inserted pinch runner Rickey Henderson, the aging speedster who'd stolen 31 bases for the Mariners after they signed him in late May. Stan Javier dropped a sacrifice bunt that moved Henderson to third with one out, and the White Sox walked David Bell.

Piniella then sent Carlos Guillen to pinch hit for catcher Joe Oliver and, like his advice to Cameron that helped win Game 1, the Mariners' skipper made a call that won the series.

"Carlos, I want you to bunt the ball, and I want you to take it right to Frank Thomas at first base," Piniella told Guillen before he walked into the on-deck circle. "He can't throw a lick, and if you get that ball down, we're going to the American League finals."

Bench coach John McLaren marveled.

"It was like George Allen designing a play for the Washington Redskins," McLaren said. "Lou is so good at that."

Foulke threw a first-pitch fastball but Guillen didn't bunt. He took a mighty swing and fouled the ball to the backstop.

In the dugout, Piniella was livid.

"Lou turned to me and said, 'What did we just tell this guy?'" McLaren said. "Lou was really steamed and he kept going on about it. He hadn't finished his next sentence and I looked up, and there was the most perfect bunt you've ever seen. I ran out of the dugout to celebrate, and Lou was still down there talking to himself."

Just as Piniella had wanted, Guillen pushed a perfect bunt toward Thomas, and Henderson scored the winning run to clinch the series.

End of story? Hardly. Four months later, when the Mariners were taking batting practice during a spring training workout, McLaren had a question for Guillen.

"Carlos, I never asked you this after the game, but do you remember when you bunted to Frank Thomas to win that game?" McLaren asked. "What happened on the pitch before that? Why did you swing?"

"Oh, I just did that on my own," Guillen said.

McLaren later told that to Piniella, who lost his cool again.

"Lou, forget about it," McLaren said. "It's over. We won the game."

Mariners Lose Their Yankees Weapon

The Mariners had to wait for their next opponent after sweeping the White Sox. The Yankees and A's took their first-round series to the limit, with the Yankees winning Game 5 to set up a Seattle-New York showdown to determine which team would play in the World Series.

During the four-day break between series, the Mariners scheduled a simulated game for left-handed starter Jamie Moyer. He hadn't pitched in the White Sox series because of tightness in the back of his shoulder, but the time off allowed him to recover, and he felt good.

Moyer's return was seen as a big edge for the Mariners if they were to face the left-handed-heavy Yankees lineup. During the regular season, Moyer was 2-0 against the Yankees with a 1.35 earned run average.

On October 7, one day after the Mariners clinched their series over the White Sox, Moyer took the mound for a 60-pitch simulated game. Through those 60 pitches, Moyer's shoulder felt fine, and he clearly was ready to face either the A's or the Yankees, whichever team won the other series.

Then he decided to throw a 61st pitch in order to work from the other side of the rubber against a left-handed hitter. Backup catcher Chris Widger, a right-handed hitter, turned around and batted left-handed. He said it was the first time he'd stood on that side of the plate since he was in high school.

Moyer then threw a pitch that may have altered the outcome of the Mariners' next series.

Widger slapped a grounder back to the mound, and the ball skipped off the grass and struck Moyer flush on his left knee. It fractured his kneecap and ended his postseason before it started. Moyer was devastated.

"It's very frustrating," he said, tears in his eyes and his voice cracking as he met the media. "I still don't believe it's over."

The Mariners, despite going 6-3 against the Yankees in the regular season, knew beating the Yankees would be an immense challenge, and without Moyer they lost a huge edge.

"I'm pretty sure it would have been a different series with him," center fielder Mike Cameron said. "He'd always done well against the Yankees, and he was the one guy who could neutralize the left-handed bats that they had—Paul O'Neill, David Justice, and Tino Martinez."

Those three hitters hurt the Mariners in the series. O'Neill batted .250 but had five RBIs in the six games. Martinez hit .320 with a home run. Justice batted .231 but hit two home runs and drove in eight runs.

No blow was bigger for the Yankees than Justice's three-run homer in the seventh inning of Game 6. The Mariners led 4-3 at the time and were in position to force a deciding Game 7 the next night.

Instead, Justice crushed a pitch from Arthur Rhodes into the upper deck at Yankee Stadium, and the Yankees went on to win 9-7 and clinch the series.

CHAPTER FIFTEEN

The Japanese Connection

WHEN SPRING TRAINING BEGAN IN 2001, Lou Piniella was worried. When was this new guy, Ichiro Suzuki, going to start pounding the baseball?

The Mariners had lost free agent Alex Rodriguez and desperately needed to replace his 41 home runs and 132 RBIs entering the 2001 season. One answer was Suzuki, the seven-time Pacific League batting champion in Japan who had signed with the Mariners to become the major leagues' first Japanese position player.

As a leadoff hitter with blazing speed, Suzuki obviously wasn't a 40-homer guy who would replace all of Rodriguez's offense. But he'd hit for good power in Japan—25 homers in 1995 with the Orix Blue Wave—and scouts said he could turn on a ball and hit it out of a ballpark with ease.

When spring training began in 2001, that wasn't the hitter Piniella saw, and it concerned him.

Suzuki, a left-handed hitter, poked every ball the opposite way, including more than a few over Piniella's head in the Mariners' third-base dugout at their Peoria, Arizona, training complex. The Mariners had invested more than $5.5 million in a batting champion, but all Piniella had seen was a skinny slap hitter who couldn't seem to get around on a spring training fastball.

"I'm worried about this kid," Piniella told his bench coach, John McLaren. "If you can't even pull the ball in spring training, you're going to have a long year."

Before an exhibition game the next day, Piniella made a simple request of Suzuki.

"I want to see you pull the ball," Piniella asked.

In his first at-bat, Suzuki smoked a line-drive single to right field and, after the inning, returned to the dugout and asked Piniella, "Is that pulling the ball OK?"

The rest of that game, Suzuki went back to his old pattern, slapping everything to the left side. All Piniella and his coaches could do was let their new player prepare for the season the way he knew best.

"Ichiro had a game plan," McLaren said. "He was learning the pitchers and staying back on the ball and hitting it the opposite way. That's how he prepared."

The rest became history.

Suzuki rolled through his first major-league season with a league-best .350 average and an incredible 243 hits. He also stole 56 bases, becoming the first player since Jackie Robinson in 1949 to lead the majors in average and steals. He became the American League MVP and Rookie of the Year, joining Fred Lynn (1975 with the Red Sox) as the only players to win those awards in the same season.

Suzuki rarely walked, but he beat out numerous infield grounders and pressured opposing defenders into mistakes because of his speed. As the best leadoff hitter in franchise history, Suzuki jump-started an offense that tore through the American League and set the Mariners on course to their record 116-victory season.

It was hardly by coincidence that Suzuki became a Mariner. The team's principal owner, Japanese businessman Hiroshi Yamauchi, is the former president of Nintendo who turned that once-small company into a giant in the video game industry.

With that connection and Seattle's standing as a Pacific Rim city that embraces its large Asian population, the Mariners saw themselves as a good fit for Japanese players. They had signed pitcher Makato Suzuki in 1993, and he remained in their system until 1999 when they traded him to the Royals.

By then, another Japanese pitcher had caught the Mariners' eye.

Ichiro Suzuki takes the field on Opening Day in 2006.
Photo by Jennifer Buchanan/The Herald of Everett, WA

Kazuhiro Sasaki, Japan's all-time saves leader, signed with the Mariners before the 2000 season and became their much-needed closer. Sasaki faced not only the pressure of the ninth inning,but also the burden of representing a nation. The curiosity in both Japan and the U.S. was considerable.

"I could sense it because there were so many interviews," Sasaki said. "I definitely felt it. But I also was able to have a lot of fun."

The attention on Suzuki became even more intense.

He had achieved rock-star status in Japan and the scrutiny didn't lessen after he became a Mariner. At his first spring training, Japanese media followed every move he made, going so far as to note where he hit each pitch during batting practice.

The Mariners got a sense of it two years earlier when they invited Suzuki to spend the early part of spring training with them in 1999 before he reported to his Japanese team, the Orix Blue Wave. The Japanese media made a big story of that every day.

Suzuki hung out with Ken Griffey Jr. and experienced some of Jay Buhner's crude pranks. He also learned a lot about the difference between baseball in the major leagues and Japan.

On Suzuki's first day with the Mariners, the team headed back to the clubhouse after their two-and-a-half-hour workout when Ted Heid, the organization's Pacific Rim scouting director, pulled McLaren aside.

"Ichiro wants to know if that's all we're going to do," Heid said.

"That's it. We're done," said McLaren, who looked up to see a puzzled expression on Suzuki's face.

"They're used to practicing five hours a day in Japan," Heid told McLaren.

After Suzuki signed with the Mariners in 2001, even more Japanese media swarmed him, both on and off the field. Photographers would arrive early in the morning, sometimes before sunrise, and station themselves at the entrance to the Mariners' parking lot, and they didn't turn their lenses away from Suzuki until he drove away after practice. Even then, some of them followed Suzuki to his apartment.

"Just looking at where he was coming from and what he brought here to Seattle, I know it had to be stressful," said Mike Cameron, the former center fielder who became a good friend of Suzuki's. "He never had a chance to unwind or relax. During that time when we were in the clubhouse by ourselves, we used that time to do that. What he did was amazing. Any time you break a barrier it can't be easy. But he not only was breaking a barrier, but he was dealing with different traditions."

The obvious question before Suzuki's first major-league season was whether he would hit as well here as he did in Japan. It didn't take him long to prove he could.

He never batted less than .312 in his first five seasons. In 2004, he batted .372 and broke one of the longest-standing records in baseball. His 262 hits broke George Sisler's single-season record of 257, set in 1920.

In 2006, Suzuki topped the 200-hit mark for the sixth straight season. Only two other players in baseball history have done better than that, Willie Keeler with eight straight from 1894 to 1901 and Wade Boggs with seven straight from 1983 to 1989.

Suzuki has admitted that he couldn't find much joy on the way to those achievements. The constant quest to set records and live up to expectations doesn't make the game as fun as it was.

"I don't know what the meaning of having fun is in baseball," he said after breaking Sisler's record. "When I go out there, as a professional, I'm not going to laugh or smile. You feel the pressure of Major League Baseball and you want to do your best, and it's hard for me to do that.

"When you're a kid, you have fun playing baseball. When you become a professional, there are responsibilities and expectations. Stepping up to the plate becomes a scary thing. In Japan, I didn't have fear. I didn't know what baseball could do to you. Here in America, I know that fear. That makes a record like this a bigger accomplishment and a bigger achievement."

CHAPTER SIXTEEN

The Record 2001 Season

AFTER THEIR PLAYOFF RUN IN 2000, the Mariners established themselves as the team to beat for the division championship in 2001. They returned a nice mixture of speed, defense, starting pitching, veteran leadership, a solid bench, and that outstanding bullpen.

The Mariners believed they were a good team. How good? Nobody quite knew.

For the second straight season, the Mariners had to replace the anchor to their offense.

In 2000, they overcame the loss of Ken Griffey Jr. This time it was shortstop Alex Rodriguez, who became a free agent and signed a 10-year, $252 million contract with the Texas Rangers. He had led the Mariners with 41 home runs and a .606 slugging percentage in 2000, plus 132 RBIs and a .420 on-base percentage that were second on the team to DH Edgar Martinez.

The greater concern in Seattle was how the M's would make up for his lost offense.

Part of the solution was Bret Boone, a free-agent second baseman whose knee problems in 2000 thwarted what had begun as a nice season offensively. Boone gave the Mariners much more than anyone expected. He hit 37 home runs, drove in 141, and narrowly missed winning the American League MVP award. He lost that

Jamie Moyer pitches against the Cleveland Indians in Game 2 of the 2001 ALDS. *Photo by Michael O'Leary/The Herald of Everett, WA*

honor to another newcomer who became an instant hit, not only in Seattle but around the major leagues.

Ichiro Suzuki, the first position player to come to the majors from Japan, became the leadoff hitter that the organization had sought from the beginning in 1977.

Suzuki used his slap-hitting approach and blazing speed to lead the league with 242 hits—most ever by a rookie—a .350 average and 56 steals. He irritated pitchers with his ability to make contact with anything in or out of the strike zone, and his speed forced opposing infielders to play him shallow, opening lanes for base hits. Once on base, he forced opponents into mistakes.

Suzuki won both the American League Rookie of the Year and MVP awards.

Boone and Suzuki became the perfect additions to a lineup that already featured the potent bats of Edgar Martinez, Mike Cameron, and John Olerud.

On the mound, the Mariners didn't have a true ace in the starting rotation, but they rolled out five starters who gave them a chance to win every day. Backed by the improved offense and the best defensive team in the league, the starters flourished. Veteran Jamie Moyer won 20 games for the first time in his career, going 20-6. Freddy Garcia went 18-6, Paul Abbott 17-4, Aaron Sele 15-5, and John Halama 10-7.

The bullpen became the strongest in team history, with Norm Charlton, Jeff Nelson, and Arthur Rhodes forming a perfect left-right-left setup for Japanese closer Kazuhiro Sasaki, who set a single-season franchise record with 45 saves the previous year.

The combination of offense, defense, and pitching carried the Mariners to an incredible 116 victories, tying the 1906 Chicago Cubs' major-league record for most victories in a season and breaking the 1998 New York Yankees' American League record of 114.

"Once we started playing in spring training, we realized we were pretty good," Cameron said. "But we didn't know we were going to be that good."

Playing a second straight year without a superstar, the Mariners succeeded because of their strength throughout the roster and manager Lou Piniella's practice of playing versatile Mark McLemore regularly while giving the starters frequent days off. Every player on that team performed a key role in the successful season, and they maintained a killer instinct that didn't wane as they built a big lead in the standings.

"We would win eight games in a row and then lose the ninth one 3-2, and guys were flat-out pissed off because they'd lost a winnable game," pitching coach Bryan Price said. "We had that rare sense over the entire season that we were going to win 100 percent of the games. At no time did we ever feel we were out of a game."

The Mariners beat Oakland 5-4 in the season opener at Safeco Field and never cooled off. They won 20 of their first 24 games in April.

Bret Boone and Mark McLemore celebrate at home plate during the
Mariners' record 116-win season in 2001.
Photo by Stephanie S. Cordle/The Herald of Everett, WA

"There were so many things we did well," Cameron said. "We
hit and pitched well, we hit with people on base and our situational
play was unreal."

When the Mariners needed a ground ball to push a runner from
second to third with nobody out, they did it without worrying
about the dip in batting average. They used the big gaps at Safeco
Field to drive extra-base hits and cut down on rally-killing
strikeouts. Most of all, they pitched well, played great defense and,
with that strong bullpen, needed only to have a lead after six innings
to virtually ensure victory.

"We could feel that other teams were weary, or maybe leery, of
playing us," Boone said. "They knew if they made a mistake, we
were going to beat them. What's incredible is that the group we had
was the farthest from being an arrogant group of guys. It was the
most humble team I'd ever played on, but it was a confident team."

Edgar Martinez, John Olerud, Dan Wilson, and Stan Javier were
the quiet backbone of the 2001 Mariners. Boone walked with a
swagger but absorbed as much needling from his teammates as he

dished out. Cameron lifted the clubhouse with his smile. And Piniella, of course, pulled it all together with his intensity.

"For years and years in my career, I never thought much of the cliché that teams click because of chemistry," Boone said. "You have good players, you win. We had a lot of talent that year, but it wasn't the greatest assemblage of talent ever. But when game time came, the attitude was, 'Let's go get 'em.' As the season wore on, it snowballed. It became clear to me that chemistry is important in this game."

The Mariners' romp continued through May and June, including a 15-game winning streak from May 23 to June 8 that raised their record to 47-12.

"Anybody who was a part of that team was blessed to be going through a season like that," Price said.

September 11: Tragedy Amid Their Greatest Triumph

The Mariners were in cruise control at the All-Star break, with a 63-24 record and a 19-game lead over second-place Oakland in the AL West. Eight Mariners made the American League All-Star team—Bret Boone, Mike Cameron, John Olerud, Edgar Martinez, Ichiro Suzuki, Freddy Garcia, Jeff Nelson, and Kazuhiro Sasaki—in a game that became a Seattle showcase. Played at Safeco Field, the AL won 4-1, and Sasaki recorded the save.

The All-Star break hardly cooled off the Mariners. They went 53-22 the rest of the season and won the division by 14 games over Oakland. The Mariners didn't lose more than two games in a row until the final month, a testament to the focus of a veteran team.

As August turned into September, only two questions remained: Would the Mariners stay hot and beat the 1906 Cubs' major-league record of 116 victories in a season? And when does the World Series start?

The Mariners could almost taste the champagne after they beat the Angels 5-1 on September 10 to begin a three-game series at Anaheim. It gave the Mariners a 17-game lead over Oakland with 18 to play, leaving them on the verge of the organization's third

American League West Division championship. Better yet, the Mariners won for the 104th time, pushing them closer to the 116-victory mark.

They went to bed that night at the Doubletree Hotel in Anaheim enjoying one of the most successful seasons a team has ever accomplished. The next morning, they woke up to horror.

Ron Spellecy, the Mariners' traveling secretary, was rattled awake by the ring of his cell phone. His girlfriend was calling from Seattle.

"Are you watching the news?" she asked.

"Hello? It's 6:30 in the morning," Spellecy said.

"Just turn on the news," she said, without telling him why.

Spellecy grabbed the clicker and turned on the TV, but he couldn't comprehend what was happening. Commentators were talking about an emergency at the World Trade Center in New York, and cameras were focused on smoke billowing from one of the twin towers.

"Just then, I saw a plane go into the second tower," Spellecy said. "I sat there thinking, 'This can't be true. Who's playing this game? It can't be happening.'"

It was, and soon Spellecy and the Mariners learned how little baseball mattered. The world changed on September 11, 2001.

Nineteen men affiliated with al Qaeda had hijacked four planes on the East Coast, crashing two of them into each of the World Trade Center's twin towers and another into the Pentagon. A fourth went down in a field in Pennsylvania, apparently headed toward the U.S. Capitol building before passengers wrestled control away from the hijackers.

Stunned by the daylong reports from the East Coast, playing a baseball game didn't seem important to the Mariners. That night's game against the Angels was called off.

"There were so many real-life things going on that were important besides baseball," Cameron said. "What happened put things in perspective to the point that the game itself wasn't important. It put a halt on all that we had accomplished to that point in the season, but what could we do? It's life we were dealing with."

The Mariners spent the day glued to the TV and wondering when they would play again. What about the final game of the

Anaheim series the next day? And the four games that were scheduled Thursday through Sunday in Seattle against the Texas Rangers? With air space closed because the threat to U.S. security remained uncertain, how would the Mariners get home for those games?

Spellecy booked a banquet room and called an afternoon meeting of players, coaches, team executives, families, and media to try to answer those questions. General manager Pat Gillick and Spellecy addressed the group, neither able to deliver a firm plan of what would happen the next few days.

"We're going to sit here in Anaheim until we know what we're going to be doing," Spellecy told everyone. "Right now, this game has been cancelled. We don't know about the next day."

On Thursday, September 13, commissioner Bud Selig announced that baseball wouldn't resume until the following Tuesday, September 18.

"When they finally made the call to postpone, that's when we said, 'Oh crap! How do we get all these people home?'" Spellecy said.

The Mariners' traveling party in Anaheim was larger than usual, with several families along to visit Disneyland.

"We lined up four buses and told everyone that we were going to leave at 11 o'clock on Friday morning and ride back to Seattle," Spellecy said. "It was going to be a 20-some-hour trip."

The Mariners didn't abandon hope of arranging a flight back to Seattle, but that seemed futile because airspace remained closed.

"I was calling all my contacts within the airline industry, but everything was cancelled, and nobody knew when they would be flying again," Spellecy said. "Then, Pat Gillick said, 'Why don't you call Alaska back?'"

Spellecy did, hoping for the off chance that Alaska Airlines would have a plane in Los Angeles that could transport the Mariners to Seattle if flights resumed. The airline's response was as uncertain that day as it had been since the 9-11 attacks. Nobody knew when airspace would reopen, and when it did, nobody knew what regulations or limitations there would be.

"That's fine," Spellecy said. "Just keep us in mind."

On Friday morning, the Mariners' equipment was loaded onto a truck and it left about 9 a.m. to begin a drive of nearly 1,200 miles to Seattle. The four buses were scheduled to arrive at the hotel about an hour later, and Spellecy held another briefing with the team to discuss the trip back to Seattle.

About 30 minutes later, his cell phone rang. It was an official from Alaska Airlines.

"We have a plane. It's at LAX and it's yours if you want it," Spellecy was told. His response was brief but emphatic.

"Yes! We want that flight!"

Just then, four buses rounded the corner and pulled onto the hotel grounds, ready for the long journey to Seattle. The Mariners used those buses, but only for the drive from Anaheim to Los Angeles International Airport.

Gillick held one last meeting to tell everyone of the change in plan—that the team would fly back to Seattle, not bus—and he emphasized that the threat to U.S. security remained uncertain and that the situation was still serious.

"If there's one practical joke or if anybody doesn't go through security, if you're carrying anything you shouldn't or if you make bad jokes, you're going to be in deep, deep trouble," Gillick said. "This is not fun and games. Have your IDs ready. Have your passports ready. Don't mess this up."

"We had to make it very, very clear to everybody flying with us how serious this was," Spellecy said.

That became apparent during the drive to the airport. Four cars from the Orange County Sheriff's Department escorted the Mariners' buses, and the freeways around Los Angeles were nearly deserted. So was LAX when the team arrived.

"It was such an eerie feeling," Spellecy said. "It was desolate going up there. Nobody was driving. We were going 70 miles an hour on the freeway, and the traffic was maybe the quietest it's ever been in L.A. I think people were staying home wondering, 'What's going to happen next?'"

The buses arrived at the airport and the Mariners entered a terminal deserted of anyone but a few airline workers and numerous law enforcement officers.

"There were police standing all over the place when we got to the airport, but even they didn't really know what was going on," Spellecy said. "We had to take our luggage and check it, but the people with the airline had no idea what was going on, either. They hadn't been working for three or four days, and then all of a sudden it's open. There was a lot of confusion, and it took us a while to get on the plane."

When the Mariners finally boarded the plane and settled in their seats, the pilot made a brief announcement before takeoff.

"We're the only plane leaving right now," he said. "Welcome aboard and let's get out of here."

The Mariners were never so glad to hear those words.

Life After 9-11

The Mariners had to get their minds back on baseball when games resumed on Tuesday, September 18. It wasn't easy.

The terrorist attacks still weighed on everyone's mind, and every jet that flew over Safeco Field on its approach to Seattle-Tacoma International Airport became a nervous reminder of what happened a week earlier.

Everyone who attended the first game back against the Angels received a small American flag, and pregame ceremonies brought tears to a lot of eyes. Between "God Bless America" and the "Star Spangled Banner," the sellout crowd broke into a loud chant of "U-S-A! U-S-A!"

Manager Lou Piniella called it a beautiful moment, and third baseman Mark McLemore was like many of the players, having to dig deep for the focus needed to play the game.

"I was pretty much a wreck until the first inning," McLemore said.

They all felt a responsibility to get back on the field and give America a diversion from what had occurred on the East Coast a week earlier.

"We were going through one of the roughest times in this country's history, and the people needed baseball as something to get their minds off everything on TV that was so negative," second baseman Bret Boone said. "I felt a responsibility as an athlete, as an entertainer, to go back to work and for three hours a night allow people to watch a ballgame and get their minds off it. That was our obligation to the country."

Pitcher Freddy Garcia did his part in the first game back, pitching a three-hit complete game in the Mariners' 4-0 victory over the Angels. That cut the magic number for clinching the division title to one—an Oakland loss or a Mariners victory would give the M's their third division championship.

That could happen the next night, and the Mariners knew that their victory celebration would be seen, and probably critiqued, nationwide. They knew it needed to be tasteful and not the raucous, champagne-spraying delirium that is common when baseball teams win championships.

"We talked for a week about how we should do it," Cameron said. "We knew we had to do it in a respectful way."

Oakland lost to the Texas Rangers, and the Mariners beat the Angels, clinching the third division championship in franchise history. When closer Kazuhiro Sasaki got Jose Nieves on a popup to Boone for the final out of a 5-0 victory, there was no massive pileup of players on the field.

Instead, the Mariners hugged each other and waved to the crowd. McLemore took an American flag and walked to the top of the pitcher's mound, waving it as his Mariners teammates gathered nearby.

"McLemore had talked a little about doing that," bench coach John McLaren said. "But the way it unfolded, it was spontaneous."

The players, coaches, and Piniella all dropped to a knee on the mound and bowed their heads for a moment of silence. The stadium fell silent, except for some who sobbed at the scene. The emotion overwhelmed Mariners utility player Stan Javier, who broke down and cried.

Then the players rose to their feet and made a slow walk around the diamond, led by McLemore with the American flag. The crowd cheered loudly, but with respect.

Relief pitcher Arthur Rhodes broke from the pack of players and ran down the left-field line, where he stopped and embraced a police officer.

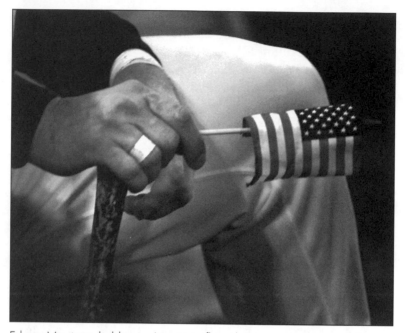

Edgar Martinez holds an American flag during pregame ceremonies at Safeco Field in 2001 when baseball resumed after the 9-11 attacks.
Photo by Dan Bates/The Herald of Everett, WA

Players took turns carrying the flag around the diamond, and when they reached home plate, Cameron and Piniella held it aloft. The players smiled, waved and then retreated to the clubhouse for their own private, but still respectfully quiet, celebration of the division title.

"We had a little champagne because we've worked hard," Piniella said. "It was subdued and it was in very good taste."

With the division championship secure and still 16 games remaining in the season, there were more important matters than an all-out effort to beat the single-season record of 116 victories. The Mariners needed to go 11-5 the rest of the way to do that, and it was entirely possible on this team, but Piniella knew it was more important to get them ready for the playoffs. The first step was to give the regulars plenty of rest in the final two weeks of the regular season.

Piniella did that, and the Mariners lost four straight, leaving them stuck on 106 victories with a dozen games remaining.

"We had to win 10 of the last 12 to tie the record," Cameron said. "I'm not sure how many in a row we won, but we were playing very, very well by the end of the season."

The Mariners won nine of the next 10, leaving them one victory from tying the record with two games remaining in the regular season. They got it in the next-to-last game, beating the Rangers 1-0 on October 6 when minor-league call-up Denny Stark led a parade of five Mariners pitchers to the mound as Piniella tuned up his staff for the playoffs.

The Rangers won the final game 4-3, scoring a run in the top of the ninth, to leave the Mariners with 116 victories.

Illness Strikes a Star

Along with their great baseball, the Mariners were blessed with good health most of the 2001 season. Injuries to front-line players were minimal.

Outfielder Jay Buhner missed all but the final month because of an injury to his left foot. Norm Charlton, Edgar Martinez and Stan Javier all spent time on the 15-day disabled list with leg issues, but they returned to play key roles in the Mariners' drive to the division championship.

Manager Lou Piniella rotated his lineup, giving starters frequent time off in order to keep everyone fresh through the heat of the summer.

It was all working well until shortstop Carlos Guillen got sick in September.

"He'd had problems off and on the whole year," trainer Rick Griffin said.

Guillen said nothing about feeling sick, but he'd experienced nosebleeds during the season and missed several games.

"The 10 days when he was really suffering, he hit over .400," Griffin said. "He could get himself through the games, but then he'd go home feeling bad, and he was coughing up blood."

Guillen underwent tests, and on September 28 his problem was diagnosed as pulmonary tuberculosis. He was hospitalized immediately and placed under quarantine because of the highly contagious disease.

"Carlos probably contracted it from someone when he was home in Venezuela," Griffin said. "He was toughing it out. But if it had gone on much longer without treatment, it could have become extremely serious."

Guillen's teammates became very worried because the disease can be spread via airborne particles, and they had spent considerable time in close quarters on flights, buses, and in clubhouses.

Every Mariner was tested for TB, and nine players tested positive, meaning they had contracted the disease although they hadn't shown symptoms of illness. Those nine, whose names were never revealed, took medication for the next nine months.

Guillen missed the rest of the regular season, plus the first-round playoff series against the Indians. He started the first game of the American League Championship Series against the Yankees but physically wasn't able to play every game of the series. He pinch hit in Game 3 and started Game 5, getting two hits in his eight at-bats in the series.

Postseason Disappointment

History said the Mariners should have reached the World Series in 2001.

Of the 23 other teams in baseball history that had won 105 or more regular-season games, only the 1998 Atlanta Braves failed to reach the World Series.

This, however, is the era of divisional play and two rounds of playoffs just to reach the World Series. No matter how successful the regular season was, it took a hot team to advance through the division series and league championship series.

The Mariners never found their regular-season rhythm in mid-October.

Perhaps it was the letdown after the push to win 116 games.

Perhaps it was the illness to Carlos Guillen.

Perhaps it was the strained oblique suffered by unsung infielder David Bell during a workout after the 9-11 attacks. Bell, who batted

.260 with 15 home runs in the regular season, hit .188 in the postseason.

Indians ace Bartolo Colon shut out the Mariners on six hits in a 5-0 victory in Game 1 of the AL Division Series at Safeco Field, but the Mariners came back the next day behind left-hander Jamie Moyer, who held the Tribe to one run. The M's scored four times in the first inning off Indians lefty Chuck Finley and held on for a crucial 5-1 victory.

Having gained a split of the two games at Safeco Field, the Indians believed they had the momentum with the best-of-five series shifting to Cleveland for Games 3 and 4.

The third game was a nightmare for the Mariners. The Indians pummeled Seattle starter Aaron Sele, who had never won a postseason game, with four runs in the first two innings and didn't let up against three Mariners relievers. The Indians won 17-2 and celebrated afterward as though they had the series in their pockets. All they needed was one more victory to celebrate in earnest.

The next day, before Game 4, Mariners CEO Howard Lincoln sat in the dugout at Jacobs Field, on the brink of seeing his magnificent team eliminated in the first round of the playoffs. What irritated him most was how the Indians reacted to their Game 3 victory.

"Those guys were jumping around yesterday like they'd already won the series," Lincoln said. "There's nothing more I would like than to beat those guys."

With their marvelous season one loss from crumbling, the Mariners rallied. They came from behind and beat the Indians 6-2 in Game 4, then clinched the series when Jamie Moyer out-pitched Chuck Finley in a 3-1 victory at Safeco Field.

The Mariners, who observed their division championship with a subdued celebration three and a half weeks earlier, sprayed champagne this time. It was their last joy.

Andy Pettitte held the Mariners to three hits in eight innings, leading the Yankees to a 4-2 victory in Game 1 of the ALCS at Safeco Field. The next night Mike Mussina beat them 3-2, leaving the Mariners in a dire hole as they prepared for the next three games at Yankee Stadium.

Reporters, waiting outside the Mariners' clubhouse before being allowed access to the players, were surprised to see Lou Piniella when the doors burst open. On his way to the required postgame press conference, he stopped and delivered a bold statement.

"Let me interject one thing," Piniella said with fire in his eyes. "We'll be back here to play Game 6! I've got confidence in my baseball club. We've gone to New York and beaten them five of six times. We'll do it again! We've got another five games to play!"

To do that, the Mariners had to win at least two of the next three games at Yankee Stadium, where they had indeed dominated the Yankees in the six regular-season games in New York.

Returning there in October, however, was different.

The Mariners were playing a Yankees team that suddenly had gained the empathy of the nation, because they represented a city that continued to suffer from the September 11 terrorist attacks.

The Mariners had the right man pitching in Game 3, Jamie Moyer, and they played their best game of the postseason. Moyer held the Yankees to two runs in seven innings, and the Mariners broke out with seven runs in the sixth inning, rolling to a 14-3 victory.

It not only pulled them back into the series, it gave the Mariners a sense of energy they hadn't shown in the postseason. The killer instinct that had been such an important part of the regular season finally had returned.

One day later, before the biggest game of their season, all of that energy seemed lost.

Piniella, his coaches, front-office executives, and several players took a bus to the site of the World Trade Center. They met firefighters at Firehouse 24, Ladder Co. 1, the home station of several who lost their lives on September 11. They met families of lost firefighters and police officers. Then they toured the ruins of the World Trade Center, smoke still drifting from the pile of twisted steel and the smell of sulfur lingering in the air.

"After seeing that, how do you put baseball in the same context?" pitching coach Bryan Price wondered. "How do you make baseball the priority? It was a very, very difficult thing for us to do."

Trainer Rick Griffin, who was on that bus, also sensed a change in the team.

"We saw first-hand the devastation," he said. "We met relatives of people who were lost. We met people who survived. We met wives of the firefighters whose husbands had been buried alive. This was a close-knit team and they were very family-oriented, and they were really affected. It took the focus away from baseball."

That night in Game 4, the Mariners and Yankees were scoreless through seven tense innings. Before the top of the eighth, second baseman Bret Boone did his best to instill a spark by giving his teammates a dugout lecture.

"If any of you want to make it to that postgame interview room, then you'd better do something this inning," Boone yelled.

Boone, the third hitter up in that inning, knew the Mariners needed to score in the eighth because they'd face the Yankees' dominating closer, Mariano Rivera, in the ninth. Ichiro Suzuki grounded out and Mark McLemore lined out, bringing Boone to the plate with two outs against right-hander Ramiro Mendoza.

Boone drove a pitch from Mendoza deep to left-center field, clearing the wall for a 1-0 Mariners lead.

With two of their best relievers ready to close out the Yankees—Arthur Rhodes in the eighth and Kazuhiro Sasaki in the ninth—the Mariners should have been in a perfect position to even the series at two victories apiece. The left-handed Rhodes would face two of the Yankees' tough left-handed hitters, David Justice and Tino Martinez, but in between them was dangerous switch-hitting Bernie Williams.

"I thought we had it in the bag then," Boone said. "But then, in that next inning when I went out to the field, it was like a weird thing was happening. The wind started swirling and I remember seeing hotdog wrappers flying around."

Rhodes struck out Justice, but he fell behind in the count to Williams before working his way back to a full count. Then Rhodes went to his best pitch, a 95-mph fastball.

Williams made contact, but not good contact, lofting an innocent-looking high fly to right-center field. It looked certain to be the second out of the inning.

"That ball was a can of corn," Boone said. "You can tell when a ball goes over your head if it's hit well, and Bernie didn't get all of it. I almost held up my hand and said, 'Two down!'"

The wind grabbed that ball and carried it over the fence, tying the score 1-1.

"Here I am thinking that ball's going to be caught close to the warning track, and it winds up five rows deep," Boone said. "That's when you start believing in the ghosts at Yankee Stadium."

Rhodes got Martinez and Jorge Posada to end the inning, and Rivera rolled through the Mariners 1-2-3 in the top of the ninth.

Sasaki took the mound for the bottom of the ninth and promptly gave up an infield single to Scott Brosius, then faced young second baseman Alfonso Soriano, who had flashed some power with 18 home runs in his first full major-league season.

Like the pitch Williams hit off Rhodes in the eighth, Soriano drove this one off Sasaki high in the air and the wind helped do the rest, carrying it over the fence in right-center to win the game, 3-1.

"That was the turning point the series," Boone said. "We win that game, we win the series. But now our backs are against the wall as much as they can be."

They never had a chance.

The Yankees scored four runs in the fourth inning of Game 5 off Aaron Sele and didn't let up. The Mariners trailed 12-3 when they batted in the top of the ninth, and the boisterous crowd at Yankee Stadium had worked itself into a frenzy.

The cheering and stomping became more intense with each out in the ninth, and the fans dished Piniella's words back at him with the chant "No Game 6! No Game 6!" When Mike Cameron lined out to end the series and send the Yankees to the World Series, fans literally shook the stadium.

In the visiting dugout, Piniella, the man who detests losing any game, anywhere, any time, absorbed the defeat with compassion for a city that had waited six brutal weeks to have something to cheer.

"About the eighth inning, when the fans were really reveling in the stands, the one thought that came to my mind was that, boy, this city suffered a lot and tonight they let out a lot of emotions," Piniella said in the postgame news conference. "I felt good for them in that way. That's a strange thought to come from a manager who's getting his ass kicked."

For all that the Mariners accomplished in the 2001 regular season, the series loss to the Yankees was a bitter disappointment, especially after they had dominated the Yanks during the regular season.

Perhaps it shouldn't have been a surprise.

The drive to 116 victories took a life of its own as the Mariners gained national exposure in trying to become one of the most successful teams of all time. By the end of the season, it wore on them.

"The media scrutiny became so heavy down the stretch that year," Boone said. "I don't want to make an excuse, but that might have been our downfall."

When the Mariners won their record-tying 116th game by beating the Rangers on the next-to-last day of the regular season, a sense of relief swept the clubhouse.

"Everybody in that room looked at each other and sighed like finally we did it," Boone said. "Then we realized, wait a minute, we've got to play the postseason now."

The postseason was a struggle and, despite the opening-round victory over the Indians, the Mariners couldn't regain the momentum that carried them through the previous six months.

"We didn't play very well against Cleveland and beat a great team," Boone said. "We didn't play very well against the Yankees, nor did they, but they got a couple of timely hits and won the series. I look back on it now and see how we came up short."

CHAPTER SEVENTEEN

Fade from Contention

THERE WAS NO GREATER TIME TO BE A BASEBALL FAN in Seattle than the seven seasons from 1995 to 2001.

The Mariners won three division championships, reached the playoffs four times, developed superstar players, and moved their artificially induced game from the Kingdome to the real grass of Safeco Field.

On the field, it seemed only a matter of time before the Mariners reached the World Series. In the stands, the Mariners drew more than three and a half million in the 2001 and 2002 seasons.

A not-so-funny thing tends to happen in baseball when teams ride their euphoria and their aging stars too long. Winners become losers, and it can happen fast.

The Mariners faded quickly from the top of the division to the bottom.

It started with injuries throughout a supposedly pitching-rich minor-league system that inhibited the Mariners' ability to make trades. They also didn't mix the veteran roster with a young player or two each year, possibly because the minors were void of major-league-ready players.

In 2002, the Mariners got older instead of younger, bringing in veterans such as catcher Pat Borders, outfielder Ruben Sierra, and utility players Desi Relaford and Jose Offerman.

They had an impressive young outfielder in the minors, Scott Podsednik, who tripled in his first major-league at-bat after he was called up in 2001. He got only 25 more major-league at-bats the next one and a half years before the Mariners lost him on waivers to the Milwaukee Brewers after the 2002 season. The next year, Podsednik batted .314, stole 43 bases and finished second in the NL Rookie of the Year voting to Dontrelle Willis.

Figuring older and wiser was better, the Mariners began the 2002 season with aspirations of going farther than they did in 2001. Some players, in fact, said during spring training that they'd consider the season a failure if they didn't reach the World Series.

Instead, the Mariners went backward. After coming so close to the World Series in 2000 and 2001 that they could measure their downfall in a few at-bats that might have made a difference, the M's haven't been to the playoffs since.

They won 93 games in the 2002 season but couldn't match the incredible run of the Oakland A's, whose 42-12 finish in the final two months included a 20-game winning streak. The Mariners also won 93 games in 2003, but Oakland surged again late in the season and the M's didn't, losing the division by three games.

The 2004, 2005, and 2006 seasons were last-place disasters.

What went wrong?

Maybe the Mariners clung to their pleasant memories too long and didn't realize how close they were to the dismal period that was ahead. Maybe they were too reluctant to part with the popular but aging players who'd provided so many good moments.

There's no doubt that age caught up with the team. Their bats got slower, their pitching softened, and they weren't able to replace the old with the new and produce similar results.

Manager Lou Piniella angered ownership with his constant complaints that the team needed more help offensively, and he was gone after the 2002 season. The Mariners essentially traded Piniella to the Tampa Bay Devil Rays, receiving outfielder Randy Winn as compensation. A year later, general manager Pat Gillick stepped down and was replaced by former Angels GM Bill Bavasi.

After Piniella, the Mariners hired former big-league catcher Bob Melvin, a kinder, gentler skipper whose only managerial experience consisted of a few weeks in the Arizona Fall League in 1999. Melvin understandably took a hands-off approach with the veteran club in 2003 and won 93 games, but the 93-loss season in 2004 cost him his job.

Bavasi brought in veteran manager Mike Hargrove, whose Indians teams dominated the American League Central Division in the 1990s. Hargrove, however, had suffered through four losing seasons as Baltimore's manager before he was fired, and nothing changed in his first two years in Seattle despite considerable change to the roster.

The 2006 Mariners, though slightly improved over 2005, still weren't a shadow of the playoff teams that fans had known so fondly.

Jay Buhner, Edgar Martinez, and Dan Wilson had retired. Mike Cameron left as a free agent. So did Mark McLemore, who played with the A's in 2004 before retiring, and John Olerud, the hometown favorite who played with the Yankees and Red Sox before retiring in 2006. The Mariners traded fading Bret Boone to the Twins midway through the 2005 season and he, too, retired, after a few days of spring training with the Mets in 2006.

Kazuhiro Sasaki, who set the franchise record with 129 saves in four seasons, shocked the Mariners when he returned to Japan before the 2004 season, forfeiting $8.5 million in the final year of his contract. Sasaki, who said he needed to be closer to his family, pitched another year in Japan before retiring.

Jamie Moyer, the soft-tossing left-hander who won more games than any other Mariner in his 10 seasons, was traded to the Philadelphia Phillies late in the 2006 season.

That left Ichiro Suzuki as the only remaining piece from the 2001 team, and around him the Mariners fielded a mixture of young players with undetermined futures and veterans with nice credentials but little history as winners. Only nine players on the 25-man Opening-Day roster in 2006 had playoff experience, and just two of those, pitcher Jarrod Washburn and DH Carl Everett, had played in a World Series. By midseason, Everett was such an offensive disappointment that the Mariners released him.

Nobody could accuse the Mariners of not spending money on their players. Before the 2005 season, they signed third baseman Adrian Beltre to a five-year, $64 million contract and first baseman Richie Sexson to a four-year, $50 million deal.

The Mariners were lured to Beltre by his phenomenal 2004 season, when he hit 48 home runs and drove in 121 with the Dodgers. However, he became a mental basket case in his first year with the Mariners, finishing with a .255 average, 19 homers, and 87 RBIs.

Sexson performed as advertised, hitting 39 homers and driving in 121. But he also maintained his penchant for striking out, fanning 167 times. Despite the impressive home run and RBI numbers, critics of Sexson said his high strikeout totals made him a poor fit for an offense that needed to play more small ball at Safeco Field.

By the end of the 2006 season, players such as 43-year-old Jamie Moyer, 36-year-old Eddie Guardado, and 35-year-old Carl Everett were gone, and the Mariners fielded the youngest roster in the majors, averaging 26.53 years.

Two of those kids, 24-year-old shortstop Yuniesky Betancourt and 20-year-old pitcher Felix Hernandez, carried the best hope for the Mariners' future, and they both arrived with wonderful stories to tell.

Yuniesky Betancourt's Harrowing Journey to the Big Leagues

Go ahead and knock Yuniesky Betancourt down with a 95-mph fastball under his chin. He's gotten up from worse.

You think sliding hard into him at second base will test his toughness? That's no measure of toughness, not after what he has experienced.

Among teammates and opponents alike, nobody's trip to the major leagues brought as much sacrifice and peril as what Betancourt endured.

The Mariners' shortstop reached the big leagues in 2005, less than two years after he risked his life fleeing Cuba. Determined to leave the grip of the Cuban government and pursue his major-league dream, Betancourt climbed into a small boat in November of 2003 and pushed off into an ocean of uncertainty.

He had starred on the Villa Clara team in the Cuban National League and, at age 17, played for Cuba's World Junior team. Betancourt dreamed of more—a career in the major leagues and a life in a free country—and he had to flee Cuba to make that possible.

Betancourt and a teammate, pitcher Saidel Beltran, planned the trip for three months and, in the middle of the night on November 28, 2003, they climbed aboard a small motorized vessel with eight others. Betancourt doesn't speak in detail about the boat or how he arranged to flee, because he fears the government would persecute family and friends back home. His mother and grandmother, who raised him, remained in Cuba.

"I didn't feel I had the liberties and freedoms I would like to have," Betancourt said. "It was something I talked about a lot with my family. It was very difficult, but I knew I had to do it so I could realize my dream.

"If they (Cuban authorities) caught me, I wouldn't be able to play baseball. They would have thrown me in jail and they would have harassed my family. I was scared. But I knew I wanted to get to the big leagues and that is what motivated me."

Betancourt spent four days at sea, once stopping on a small island because the water became so rough. They landed in Cancun, Mexico, where Betancourt resumed his baseball workouts and prepared for tryout camps.

Pat Gillick, the Mariners' former general manager, had been impressed with Betancourt when he saw him playing for Cuba at the World Junior Games in 2000 in Canada. Mariners scouts saw him two years later at the World Games in Taiwan, then lost track of Betancourt.

"He disappeared from the radar for a while," said Benny Looper, the Mariners director of player development. "We didn't know what had happened to him."

Betancourt resurfaced at a tryout camp in Los Angeles, and the Mariners invited him to their training complex in Peoria, Arizona, for a closer look. They signed him early in 2005, sent him to their Double-A team in San Antonio and watched him adapt much faster than anyone anticipated.

The Mariners, thinking Betancourt would need at least one full season in the minors, promoted him to Triple-A Tacoma after 52 games, then called him up to the majors on July 28.

He tripled in his first major-league plate appearance, batted .256 in 60 games, and shows signs of becoming the Mariners' best defensive shortstop since Omar Vizquel in the late 1980s.

The Mariners became so convinced that Betancourt is their long-sought answer at shortstop that they shuffled some of the top minor-league prospects, moving former first-round draft pick Adam Jones to center field in 2005 and trading away highly regarded minor leaguer Adrubal Cabrera in 2006.

Betancourt, despite the risk he took and concerns for the family he left behind in Cuba, is achieving his dream.

"It was the right decision for me to do this," he said.

Felix Hernandez, the Boy Pitcher Who Would be King

Pat Rice, the Mariners' minor-league pitching coordinator, traveled to Venezuela in 2002 to take a look at a young pitcher named Felix Hernandez, who scouts had been raving about.

Rice and Benny Looper, the Mariners director of player development, had Hernandez throw some fastballs, and he impressed them with how the ball exploded out of his hand.

"Go ahead and throw some breaking balls," Rice told the youngster, who'd already been nicknamed "King Felix."

The kid threw a few 12-to-6 curveballs, the kind with the sharp downward break as if they were falling off a table, and Rice stood in awe.

"That wasn't just a high school curveball. It was filthy," Rice said, amazed that a high school senior already had the kind of stuff that could get major-league hitters out.

"Pat," someone told him. "Felix isn't a senior. He's a 15-year-old freshman."

Stunned, Rice could only imagine how good the kid would become in just a few years. The Mariners signed Hernandez later that summer, then brought him into their minor-league system two

Starting pitcher Felix Hernandez yells as he records the final out during a game against the Yankees in 2005. *Photo by Jennifer Buchanan/The Herald of Everett, WA*

years later as a 17-year-old. He climbed rapidly, overpowering hitters at every level, before the Mariners gave him 12 big-league starts at the end of the 2005 season.

Hernandez's record was nothing special, 4-4, but his 2.67 ERA spoke to his ability to dominate major-league hitters, even at age 19, with a 95-mph fastball and that wicked curve. He had the stuff to become a true staff ace, possibly as early as 2006, but the Mariners knew better.

They not only placed Hernandez at the back of the rotation, where expectations hopefully wouldn't seem as intense, they decided to institute a firm limit on the number of innings Hernandez would throw: 200, including the 14 he worked at spring training.

The Mariners also issued an edict to their marketing department that the "King Felix" nickname had to go, again to ease any undue expectations. (Funny, though…at spring training those words were embroidered into his glove.)

The Mariners' would-be king struggled at times and dazzled at others in his first full season, loping along with a .500 record and an ERA in the 4.60 range. The club seemed fine with that, knowing that 2006 was a season for Hernandez—along with all of the young players—to settle in as a major leaguer.

The Mariners see Hernandez as the key player in their return to prominence. They were willing to suffer through growing pains to achieve a future that reflects their success of the past.

They entered the 2007 season hoping Hernandez would take another step toward his lofty expectations. He pitched inconsistently in his first full season, going 12-14 record with a 4.25 ERA, but reported to spring training in 2007 weighing 20 pounds lighter and determined to become the Mariners' much-needed ace.

EPILOGUE

ONE OF THE BEAUTIFUL ASPECTS OF BASEBALL is that it's a daily drama that offers constant hope for a better outcome. There's always the opportunity to throw a more effective pitch to the next hitter, win the next day's game and finish higher in the standings the next season.

In their early years, hope was just about all the Mariners had.

The simple task of a .500 record was an accomplishment to celebrate, and it took the Mariners 15 years to do it. The 1995 Mariners, who won the organization's first division championship under manager Lou Piniella, were a far cry from the first team in 1977, when Darrell Johnson and his coaches had to pluck rocks from the field just to have a decent spring training practice.

The 18 years before the Mariners' success of 1995 comprised a period of frustrating finishes, players who became fan favorites and, of course, characters who made life interesting amid the losses.

Along the way, however, something marvelous happened. The Mariners built their history in Seattle.

Yes, there was the futility of the last-place teams and ownership problems that stirred fears the Mariners would move to another city. In time, however, the Mariners developed star players and competitive teams that their fans would cherish.

There was no better six-week period for the Mariners than their Refuse to Lose autumn of 1995, no more satisfying year than 2001 when they tied the major-league record with 116 victories, no more loved players than Edgar Martinez, Jay Buhner, and Dan Wilson.

Then again, there was no bigger letdown than when the magic ran out in 1995 in the American League Championship Series loss to the Indians. Or when the Yankees eliminated the Mariners in the 2001 ALCS, crumbling what seemed like a sure trip to the World Series. Or when idolized players like Martinez, Buhner, and Wilson retired, perhaps the surest sign that the game moves on, and those who get too wrapped up in the past will struggle for glory in the future.

Since 2001, the Mariners have tailspun their way back to where they were. They entered the 2007 season with three straight last-place finishes, seemingly no closer to a championship than they were 20 years earlier.

The Mariners, however, fielded a collection of promising young players such as Felix Hernandez, J.J. Putz, Adrian Beltre, Yuniesky Betancourt, and Jose Lopez, plus phenomenal leadoff hitter Ichiro Suzuki.

That's baseball, remember. It's where the next pitch delivers hope, the next game a chance at victory, the next season an opportunity to win it all.

INDEX